Danny White

Spotlights & Shadows

with daughter Heather Jo Kennedy

2024

Danny White: Spotlights and Shadows
Copyright © 2024
All rights reserved

Line/Content Editor: Janelle Evans
Interior Design: Janelle Evans
Formatting: Janelle Evans
Cover Design: Heather Jo Kennedy

1. Biography & Autobiography/ Sports
2. Family & Relationships/ General
3. Sports & Recreation/ Football

ISBN: 979-8-9901489-1-8   Hardcover
ISBN: 979-8-9901489-0-1   Trade Paperback
ISBN: 979-8-9901489-2-5   E-Book

CP

Cascade Publishing LLC

Published and Printed in the United States of America

1 2 3 4 5 6 7 8 9 10

Lessons from the Spotlights and Shadows of life in the public eye.

Former Dallas Cowboys Quarterback, Danny White, and his daughter, Heather Jo Kennedy, share authentic perspectives of celebrity family life and the wisdom gleaned from stepping away.

Table of Contents

FAITH

Forward

"This book is a treasure of stories from the good old days, but more than just stories, Danny and Heather share valuable insights about things that matter most.

Their two perspectives, Danny's often from the spotlight and Heather's from behind the scenes, give true glimpses into the peaks and valleys of celebrity life. Both, as professional coaches in their own fields, and with unique experience, turn these stories into priceless lessons others would miss.

Whiz (that's what I call Danny because his Dad's nickname was Whizzer) mentions me several times but it should be noted, I'm a fan of Danny White's too. He was one heck of a football player. Sometimes, in the off season, we would work out together. He was a great competitor. I knew if I missed a beat, he'd take over, so he kept me on my toes. At thirty-eight years old and with some injuries, I had the feeling I needed to retire but I didn't want to let my team down. With him waiting, I knew we had a great quarterback. I would not have retired if he hadn't been there.

Whiz and I had a lot of fun competing and playing the game, but what made our relationship special was our mutual understanding that football really was just a game. We were both committed to something deeper off the field. He always believed that, even though he spent significantly more time developing his skills as a quarterback, his faith in God and his family was infinitely more important. I feel the same way.

1

This book displays those commitments perfectly as it shows collaboration between father and daughter. It places the importance of faith and family above all else. It will make you laugh and tug at your heart. It will inspire you to be better."
~Roger Staubach~

Introduction

"All the variety, all the charm, all the beauty of life is made up of light and shadow."

Leo Tolstoy

The fame of football placed me squarely in the spotlight, but celebrity was never what I wanted. I played football because I loved the game and wanted to be the best I could be. I achieved fame and fortune in the world of entertainment, but my goals were driven by football excellence alone. The fame was necessary collateral damage if you will. I was not a traditional entertainer like a movie star, or a musician, but an athlete. I wanted to be a great football player, not a movie star. That said, being a celebrity certainly had its benefits but was a very uncomfortable arena for me, and one I was not trained for.

The day I retired as a player in the National Football League, I began to slowly eliminate the desire for temporary successes and replace it with a desire for more permanent elements. I just wanted to blend back into normalcy with my family and friends. Easier said than done, especially when you play the most visible position on one of the most visible teams in the world of sports. Since making the decision to retire, the journey down the ladder of fame has been very difficult at times, and I experienced periods of fog and darkness. Striving for meekness when you've been placed on a pedestal is at the very least, challenging. But I was guided and supported by family and friends, for whom I will always be extremely grateful.

Fame and fortune are admirable and desirable goals

in this life. However, they are also temporary in terms of our eternal existence. Thus, the picture on the cover of this book. The Super Bowl ring in the photo represents these high but temporary achievements. The old saying, "You can't take it with you" applies here. My wedding ring, on the other hand, (literally and figuratively) represents for me something more permanent. A bond that will never be broken given the right conditions. My Super Bowl ring is much more pleasing to the eye, but has much less significance than my wedding ring, which has a value of infinitely greater worth to me. The journey from the world represented by one ring to the world represented by the other, is the theme of this book.

After my playing career of fifteen years (two with the Memphis Southmen Grizzlies and thirteen with the Cowboys), I enjoyed a fifteen-year career as a coach in the Arena Football League and then a thirteen year career as a radio broadcaster, gradually stepping out of the spotlight. I believe in a God who wants me to gain experience, wisdom, and qualities which will help me serve Him and others and return to heaven to be reunited with those I have loved most in this life.

I have never been comfortable being a celebrity and promoting myself as if to say to the world, "I am special, and I have something important to say." But I have been haunted by the thought that I have been greatly blessed with experiences and opportunities very few get to have, experiences which taught me countless valuable lessons. How many young kids dream of being the quarterback for the Dallas Cowboys? I've lived a life most people only dream of.

That thought made me feel obligated to share some messages few others have the perspective to share. I'm not a writer, so I decided the best person to help me share those messages is one who's been at my side through the glory days and since.

It's been so natural to collaborate with my daughter Heather. As a teenager, she *almost* convinced her mother and I that she knew everything. She has since developed a great talent for expressing herself. Heather is extremely gifted. She's a wonderful artist and musician, not to mention her athletic skills. Through her current work as a life coach, speaker, wife, and mother of four, she is probably more qualified to write this book than I am.

Growing up, Heather was the most competitive person in our family, and never settled for anything other than her very best at everything she did. As an adult, she could have done any of these things professionally from the beginning but chose rather to serve her family and her fellow man by completing a full-time mission for her church and then marrying a man who she knew would be a great provider for her and the family they decided to start right away. She has since become a business manager, a homemaker, and been a leader and teacher in her church—all while raising four beautiful children and motivating her tired, old dad almost on a daily basis to write a book. I know she is constantly influenced and inspired by her mother, who is busy preparing our final home in the next life. Needless to say, I am very very proud of my little girl.

Telling these stories and sharing the insights we've gained is our way of giving back to a world that has been very generous to us.

Danny White

The thing about a spotlight is, it casts a strong shadow. An unavoidable darkness is linked to a celebrity's gleam, and I got comfortable there. So for my instinctively private self, writing a book feels like an exposé in all the worst ways. Having spent my formative years under the Texas Stadium lights with the rest of the Dallas Cowboys families, I occupied a unique situation wedged between *celebrity* and *nobody*. It was an exclusive perspective that afforded me insight to two worlds with more common ground than you'd think.

We've been nagging Dad for years to write a memoir. We collected the stories and lessons, but he was never fully on board until I began adding my voice and insight.

People ask me what it was like being the only daughter of a high-profile NFL QB, arguably one of the most scrutinized professional athletic positions in the US. As a child, I had no comparisons — it was all I knew. But as an adult and parent of my own children, I can recognize how that exposure to fame, with all its lights and shadows, shaped me. I pray what we've learned may be of worth.

Heather Jo

Preface — Down the Ladder

HJ

"Well, I took a few more steps down the ladder today," Dad casually mentioned to me over the phone. We'd been chatting for a few minutes about kids' ball game schedules and when he was coming for a visit.

"Oh no. What happened, Dad?" He knew I'd understand right away. This idea of climbing *down* a ladder has been his personal life analogy for the past several months as we've been documenting his history.

He explained that he just attended an event where an award in his name was being presented. He received no invitation to the event and had to purchase a guest ticket even to attend. There was no mention of him, no honor or accolades even as the "Danny White Award" was announced. There was no acknowledgement of his presence at all. Dad wasn't upset really, just struck by the contrast of his present circumstances in comparison to where he'd been only a few years prior.

DW

It's been said that when you're climbing a ladder you should make sure it's leaning against the right tree. When you think of using a ladder, you imagine going "up". The word "climb" typically implies ascent. But over the past several years, I have been focused on a "climb down the ladder of fame". Anyone who's used a ladder or come down a mountain knows the climb down is often the more treacherous one. It took a miraculous combination of hard work and good fortune to reach the top of the ladder in the sports realm. I spent five or six incredible years at the pinnacle of the football world. Stepping out of the spotlight and coming down from that place of high celebrity has been a struggle, but I've found myself another ladder and am fully engaged in a new climb up. I'm certain this next ladder is leaning against a more sustainable and fulfilling tree.

FAMILY

Moms

HJ

Only a quarter of a mile separated the tiny house on Ashland Street where Dad was born, from the four-bedroom brick rambler on Seventh Place, where the family moved when he was ten. But that quarter mile in Mesa, Arizona was all the world an active, growing boy needed. When school got out at Edison Elementary, he was off to those welcoming streets, his own domain.

The White Family kids, Danny, Teresa, Tammy, Cristall, and Chad were the original gang. And as the oldest brother, Dad was destined for leadership. But even leaders have a boss.

As a kid, he thought his mom was brutal. She was responsible for just about everything as far as his life was concerned, with firm support from his dad who never argued with her when it came to priorities. Whether it was homework, reading the scriptures, completing Boy Scout merit badges, or just about anything else he was involved in, she controlled it.

Once time, Dad sat on the couch all night in his baseball uniform because he was supposed to work on a merit badge before a game and didn't do it. He thought there was no way she would let him miss the game, but he was dead wrong. In his attempt to wait her out, he only found her to be relentless and apparently a lot tougher than he was.

Those childhood memories of his mom are priceless. This is one of our favorites.

DW

At five years old, I begged her to let me take piano lessons. At five and a half, I begged her to let me quit. If I'd gotten my way, I never would have learned to play the piano. But she was immovable, forcing me to learn how to play the piano. She would often march outside and call me to come in and practice when I was out playing ball. She had a rule: I couldn't play with my friends after school until I had practiced the piano for a half hour.

One summer day, we were playing a game of football with Ashland Street as the field. In the middle of the game, from our house all the way down the street, I could hear her calling my name. Busted. I knew what she wanted. I hunched down in the huddle, but her voice kept getting closer and closer. Finally, I had to face the inevitable. I had lost the battle. So embarrassing.

We were just about to score, which only made it

worse. There were only a few yards between us and the stop sign at Ashland and Sixth Street, which was the goal line, and the biggest kid on the whole block was on our team! I had it all worked out. I knew all I had to do was give her the ball a couple of times and we would score. That's right, my neighbor Joyce was the biggest kid on the block in the sixth grade. None of that mattered to Mom, though.

Forced to leave the game, I stomped into the house and plopped down at the piano, taking my frustration out on the keys. Triumphant, Mom went into the kitchen to do the dishes.

Shortly after, I heard a knock at the front door just a few feet away, but I was so angry I refused to get up to answer it. Actually, I was enjoying trying to knock the ivory off the keys. After several attempts with no response, a man opened the door, stuck his head in and yelled over my loud playing, "Hey, little boy, is your mom home?"

I stopped banging on the piano and looked out the window at the kids playing football, then back at him. "Mister, what do you think?"

After eight long years of piano lessons, I finally won the war with my mom. She made me promise that even though I didn't have to take lessons any more I would continue to play. To this day, I've kept that promise.

It's amazing to me how much this impacted my life and my career. In my rookie year with the Cowboys, our strength and conditioning coach, Bob Ward, gave me a skills test. I sat at a computer with paddles on my hands and feet for a test that measured my reaction time. It calculated the time it took me from seeing something on a screen to tapping paddles. Right hand, left foot, both feet, and so on. It logged how many I could get correct in thirty seconds. After the test, he looked at me with his mouth open and asked me specifically if I played the piano. I replied yes but questioned what that had to do with the test.

"When you play the piano you look at marks on a page and your eyes send a message to your brain, which sends a message to your body (fingers), and you react to what you see," he said. "The faster you can react to what you see, the better piano player you are (Anyone who reads music knows this to be true) and the more effective you are on this particular test."

I asked what this had to do with playing football, particularly quarterback.

He explained further, "When you play quarterback and you see something on the field (an open receiver), your eyes send a message to your brain, which sends a message to your body, and you react to what you see. The quicker you can react (get the ball to the receiver before the defense can get there) the better quarterback you are. I have found that piano players have quicker reaction times than other people, and you've proved my point. You just shattered the Cowboys record for this test."

I thought to myself, Mom always thought she was developing a piano player but had no idea how she was shaping a football player. Moms, somehow, and sooner or later, are *always* right.

Playing the piano has been a great blessing in my life in many ways. It honed my skills as a quarterback. Countless times, it's been a source of strength and therapy for me when I have needed it.

But above all, the biggest benefit from my years of playing and practicing playing the piano was the discipline that it developed. I learned to do something I didn't want to do, simply because I knew it was the right thing to do. Practicing the piano every day after school while my friends were outside playing took discipline. I didn't realize it at the time but that's really what discipline is — doing the right thing even though you don't want to do it. And to be good at anything will require some amount of it. Seeing my friends play outside while I sat at the keyboard, took a huge amount of it.

All of us develop talents during our lifetime. Some are permanent. Others, temporary. No longer do I throw footballs for a living, but I play the piano almost every day. Thank you, Mom."

HJ

You can probably imagine the kind of parent Dad became with regard to music lessons for his own children. Thirty minutes a day of practice, with no exceptions. I echo the sentiment, "Brutal!" But to this day, my brothers and I play almost every day, and music has been a valuable tool in all our lives as well. And as he stated, the discipline we developed is probably the bigger tool.

As I've coached people on finding their talents and reflected on my own hobbies and interests over the years, I've come to understand critical things about talents and gifts. Gifts are innate, talents are developed. Gifts also have inherent longevity, as this example of Dad's piano skills illustrates. Talents often have their season.

Football was a talent for Dad. He was successful in sports because he worked very hard and had some rare opportunities, which opened doors for him. A talent requires significant effort and is developed when an *ordinary ability* is given *exceptional opportunities*.

A gift requires little effort and is cultivated when an *ordinary opportunity* meets an *exceptional ability*. There is no doubt for anyone who has heard Dad play the piano, he has a gift. If you want to know what your gifts are, start with your family.

Shirley White might have known her firstborn was bound for football. At seven months pregnant with him, she was in the Chicago Bears' stadium at the final game of the 1951 season watching her favorite running back—soon-to-be father—Wilford "Whizzer" White. A brawl broke out in the snowy stadium and the crowd huddled around her to protect her. Immediately after the game, she and Grandpa started the long drive home to Arizona.

Not long after he was born, she saw a different, innate ability in Dad she knew needed cultivating. She also understood how music (and discipline) would bless his life long after his career in sports was over, because it was an inherent gift. Like a lot of moms—boy was she right.

Grandma passed away early in 2024. At ninety-four years old she was still tougher than her oldest boy, who lived only a couple miles away. He visited her regularly and she lit up when she saw him, as she always had.

We are all a product of the people surrounding us, and that includes our heritage. I would be remiss if I didn't acknowledge that I truly won the lottery in the family department. In particular, my grandparents, on both sides, were very present in my youth and had a tremendous influence on my growth. Not only directly, but indirectly by the way they parented my parents. I didn't fully appreciate that influence growing up but looking back, I sure have been lucky.

Whizzer

HJ

Danny White's biggest fan was his father, my grandpa. Whizzer never missed a game or even a practice of any sport his son was involved in, and he was involved in all of them — baseball, basketball, football, and track, all the way through high school. They would leave a baseball game and Dad would jump in the back of the car to change into his track uniform on the way to a track meet while Grandpa drove. Whatever it took to support his boy, he was all in.

DW

My father and I were always competing around the house in something — ping-pong, pool, basketball, or just playing catch in the backyard. He never talked much about his own career, so I had to learn about it from other people who raved about what a great athlete he was.

I loved hearing stories from his childhood. The following is from his own journal.

"The way they called us to school was by ringing a bell. They had a big bell tower with a rope hanging down from the bell with knots tied in it where they would grip it. They would pull and swing that big, big, iron bell, and you could hear that gong for miles.

One day at school, when I was in the 8th grade, before the noon break at school, Mr. Longdon, the principal, came into our class and asked for me to go with him to the office. I figured I was in some kind of trouble, so I reluctantly went with him. He said, "We have a problem, Wilford, and we think you can help us."

I said, "What did I do?" I was very defensive.

"Well the rope in the bell tower broke, and we can't ring the bell for the students to go out to lunch. We need someone to climb up the roof and ring the bell, and we know you can do it because we've heard you ringing it on the weekends!" So I had to shimmy up the corner of the school which had a porch-like slatted, shingle roof. Something I'd climbed at least a dozen times.

I climbed up on top of the roof. I could barely reach the bell when I put my arm through the levers on top. With my fingers barely touching the bell, I pushed it just as much as I could. Each time the bell would come back, and I would push it a little harder, until I got it going enough to really ring the bell.

So, I rang the bell, shimmied down the corner, went back in, and they didn't even say thank-you."

Wilford

DW

This is my favorite football picture of my dad. They were just starting to wear face masks, but he refused to wear one because he said it made him look like a sissy. His uniform is covered with blood (his own because he had broken his nose earlier in the game). One guy has three fingers in Dad's eye, and the other guy is reaching over Dad's shoulder. He caught this ball for a touchdown, and every time I look at it, I am reminded of how much the game, the players, and our entire culture have changed.

I think my favorite story of him as an athlete was when he competed in the Luke Greenway track meet in 8th grade at Alma Middle School. At first, his dad objected since it was forty miles across the valley and would take up the entire day. His dad relented on the condition that he found his own ride to the meet since there wouldn't be a bus. So Dad went down to the corner and hitch-hiked from Mesa over to West Phoenix to compete against all the other schools in the valley. When he got there, he entered every event they would let him enter. All he had to eat was a milkshake he bought with a dime his mother had given him for lunch.

"After lunch (the milkshake), I had to run the 440. I ran that 440 and there was just no way I would let anyone beat me so I just gutted myself and I won it, but I got so sick afterward I threw up that chocolate milkshake all over the place."

Wilford

He was pretty upset about wasting that dime. But after competing in every event he could, including the high jump, long jump, sprints and distance races, Alma School ended up taking 3rd place in the meet. Dad was the only athlete there from Alma School.

My senior year, I was a key part of all of those sports at Westwood High School. I ended up second in the state in the long jump, with my best jump ever of 23'4", a Westwood School Record. I was named most valuable player in four sports. Those were truly special years for me. My "good ol' days!"

I can recall clearly the excitement I had as a child watching my dad compete. Church softball and basketball were especially what I lived for. I would go to the games hoping a fight would break out, which it usually did. I liked the fights because my dad often would be right in the middle of them. He was a pretty competitive guy and everybody loved to get into it with him because he was a former professional football player for the Chicago Bears. He played for four years with legendary coach George Halas before he blew out his knee and had to retire.

It was especially fun when they didn't have enough guys because then I would get to join. I got to play shortstop when I was eight or nine years old on the local men's softball team. What a thrill.

HJ

At eighty-five years old, no one ever guessed his age accurately. He tussled with his grand and great-grandkids on the regular–and won. He was mischievous to the end, a serial prankster, and we loved it. Though he and Grandma had celebrated sixty-two anniversaries, we lost this tough guy too suddenly. No one saw it coming. He'd taken himself to a routine doctor's appointment and when he got back into the exam room, laid his head down to rest and never woke up. He'd mowed his lawn and loaded the mower into a truck bed that very morning.

After the shock and grief of that loss wore off, I remember talking to my dad about the way Grandpa died. His perspective was unique and comforting, "He never really had to feel old. He didn't have to say goodbye to weepy family members, he just checked out. Where can I get that ticket? No one had to take care of him, feed him, bathe him, or clothe him. That would have been really hard for him."

Hanging from my car's rearview mirror is a tiny harmonica. I keep it there as a memorial of my favorite prankster. I never, truly ever saw him without a harmonica...or two or three. And he was a genius with them, I would argue the best in the world. We never found a song he couldn't play. His daughters professionally recorded him playing some of the favorites. When I put that album on, it's like he's in the room. He's become immortal that way.

Priorities

HJ

What most people don't realize is that Whizzer's influence on my dad was much stronger off the field and off the topic of sports entirely. A single event early in Dad's life had a profound effect on his future decisions, ultimately changing the course of his career and life. It was a Sunday morning.

DW

Knowing how supportive my father was made it especially meaningful one Sunday morning, when after a late Saturday night road game, I slept in and missed church. I was in the family room watching TV when the rest of the family came home. He asked me to come back to the bedroom with him. I knew what he wanted to talk about because it was a Sunday ritual. He would want to know everything about the game—he had a million questions after every game and wanted to know why we did this, why we did that, and what I was thinking. We analyzed just about every play from the game this way.

But I was mistaken. That was not what he wanted to talk about. I sat down on the bed, and he looked me in the eyes and said, "The next time a sport interferes with church, you're going to give up sports." I felt like someone hit me in the face with a brick. I knew what a fan he was, so his message really stuck. Needless to say, I didn't miss any more church meetings, no matter how late I got home on Saturday night (or Sunday morning).

HJ

Those darn piano lessons. After college I actually taught them for many years. Sometimes, when a student was ready to stop taking lessons, parents would justify the decision to quit with the reasoning that they didn't want to force their kids to do something they didn't want to do. I knew that was just an excuse. Of course they forced their kids to do things they didn't want to do. I mean I hope most parents do! We send them to school every day, don't we? Have them make their beds, wear their coats, take their vitamins? Part of the guardian-code is making sure your kids wear their seatbelts when they don't want to. I know I benefited greatly from my parents' tougher style of parenting and by the fact that my brothers and I did an awful lot of things we didn't want to do. It's preparation for being a responsible, resilient adult.

Each weekday, I had to practice the piano first thing in the morning. In fact, I wasn't allowed to leave for school until I practiced my full thirty minutes. (How dumb was I? I remember being in college and looking back to those grade school days, wondering why I didn't just boycott piano practice and take a sick day from school. Mom and Dad must've had something on me because I do recall a heavy determination to not miss that morning bus!)

Clearly, music was a strong focus in our home, falling behind sports and social time in our family's priorities. These priorities were established from a young age by my parents, who came from similar disciplines. Religion was another focus, and my brothers and I are all still devout in our worship.

Basic economics teaches us it's wise to invest in the things that will last the longest. It would be impossible to count the hours Dad devoted to his athletics, but his parents instilled healthy prioritization habits, and to this day, faith, family, and music have played a much more significant role in his life than sports. Thankfully, my parents did the same.

As we grow up and develop our own interests it's beneficial to have the habits in place that support prioritization. Those balancing skills prevail when our parents' demands give way to our own goals and values. When people are feeling unfulfilled or frustrated with their life, there's almost always a misalignment between their values and their focus. They focus more on things that matter less, and focus less on things that matter more.

The word *focus* rather than *spend time* is intentional verbiage here. If family is your highest priority, it's unrealistic to spend all your time with them or even for them. That's unhealthy anyway! As the piano lessons illustrated, responsible and resilient adults have learned how to spend a good amount of time (if not a majority) doing things they don't necessarily *want* to do. But first priorities should dominate focus.

Time is a good indicator of focus, but the two are not synonymous. Our family dynamics taught us to examine what our values are, then make sure our focus supports it. It's okay to spend time making a living and paying the bills, but if it becomes your focus, you'll be traumatically unfulfilled when the season ends.

Jo

DW

My sophomore year in high school, a new family from Canada moved into the house behind us. At sixteen years old this didn't mean much to me...at first.

Not too long after they moved in, we had a church dance and one of our youth leaders kept trying to get one of us boys to dance with the new girl. He came up to me and personally tried to get me to dance with her. She was a really cute girl, but I had my eyes set on the platinum blonde girl everybody wanted to dance with. That first opportunity I had to interact with Jo Lynn I regrettably turned down. Thankfully, it would not be the last.

A short while later we stood out by the parking lot as

she was about to get into her car to go home. She drove a little black Volvo sports car. That got my attention. Something came over me and the words, "If you'll let me drive your car, I'll buy you a hamburger," tumbled out.

That was the beginning of the greatest relationship of my life. Homecoming was approaching and I asked her to be my date. I was the quarterback of the football team and a junior at Westwood High School. Jo Lynn had gone to two years of high school in Canada, where they only have three years of high school, so technically, she was a senior, though six months younger than me.

The first event of the evening was the football game. Early in the game, while playing defense, I came up to make a tackle at the same time as one of my teammates. His foot collided with my head and knocked me out cold. The doctors examined me and said I definitely had a concussion and that I should try to stay awake and shouldn't attempt to drive anywhere.

After I got home, I sat in the family room watching TV when Mom walked in and reminded me, "Don't you have a date with that new girl tonight?"

I said I had no idea, since I couldn't remember anything that happened that entire week. She called Jo Lynn's mom and sure enough, Jo Lynn had been waiting for me for quite some time to pick her up.

She wasn't much of a football fan and hadn't even gone to the game, so she had no idea what had happened to me. At that point it was about eleven o'clock at night, but I got dressed and my dad drove me over to her house since I couldn't drive. After we picked her up, he drove us to Bob's Big Boy on Main Street in Mesa. He sat out in the car while Jo and I went in and got that hamburger I promised her.

We then drove back to her house where, according to her, I went into their house and met her entire family. She also claims that she kissed me good night on their front doorstep when I left—a claim that I have never been able to confirm nor deny, since the next morning I couldn't remember anything that happened the whole evening.

I must have done or said something right because that night led to forty-six years of marriage, four incredible children, and sixteen grandchildren, as well as an eternal companionship. It was a very special night, but unfortunately one I will never be able to remember—at least not in this life.

HJ

She never missed an opportunity for a kiss. There were many times near the end of Mom's life that she was unresponsive to us. But somehow, even in her lowest state of consciousness, she would sense when Dad was coming in for a kiss and would pucker. It was precious. She couldn't open her eyes or respond to us vocally but, when Dad's face was near, she sensed him. Like it was her simplest form of communication. We called them 'ESP kisses.'

It's impossible to summarize the life and influence of Jo Lynn White. She was quiet and submissive but absolutely unashamed of her convictions and would put you in your place if challenged. When we got in trouble with Dad, it was a learning experience—a lesson and a lecture. When we got in trouble with Mom, it was soul crushing. We avoided it at all costs, but she had a way of walking us through our mistakes and lifting us out of them as better humans. The ultimate hostess, she provided comfort to all those around her.

We didn't get bailed out. She and Dad made us face our mistakes head-on. I thank them *now* for that. As a kid who had a tendency to leave things to the last minute, it didn't bode well for me at the time.

There was one exception I can recall. When I was ten years old, I remember being absolutely exhausted with commitments. I'd finished all my chores, practices, and activities for the day and still had one more math assignment to complete. She told me to set it on my desk and just go to sleep. I could get up early and finish before school. Waking early, I went to my desk and found the math assignment completed for me. The handwriting was much fancier than mine and the answers weren't all correct (math wasn't her forte), but it was done. The relief I felt I have never forgotten. It was her small way of showing grace when she knew I'd done my best. And it was exactly what I needed.

As children do, we used to ask her which one of us was her favorite. Her answer was always the same, "Dad." Their love was next level. It wasn't always easy or even pleasant. They had some tough times, especially through Dad's celebrity. She didn't fit in with the other players' wives and felt the weight of that rejection often. They had four kids, and as kids do, we took our toll on the family. There were financial struggles and family issues. She had a light about her that sometimes got lost in his shadow, but she never stopped shining, loving, and giving. She held him up for over forty years, truly the wind beneath his wings.

One of the greatest values Mom exemplified was humility. She powered through those difficult times, not by pride but by conviction. God came first and she gave her life over to Him by staying true to family, serving others, and serving Him. Tirelessly. She took care of herself very well, no doubt. But her confidence and composure came from something deeper.

In current times it's never been easier to dismiss

our devotions. The myriad of voices telling us to put ourselves first is impossible to ignore. But 'focus on number one' leaves little space for service to others. And service to others is where we truly find ourselves and our sustenance. That was Mom's secret. She was a giver, even in her subconscious ESP kisses.

High School

HJ

Dad was involved in student government and enjoyed all the activities that arose at Westwood High School, but above all he was a star in the sports realm as a four-sport athlete, and a high performer in all of them.

Still, he was not highly recruited out of high school. His sophomore year, he broke the middle finger on his right hand while making a tackle and had to play wide receiver. His junior year, he got kicked in the head trying to make a tackle and got a concussion, which put him out for the entire year. His senior year was an average season for the team. They had a decent record at 9-1 but lost their last game and didn't make the playoffs.

DW

I did okay my senior year in high school but was not stellar as a quarterback, so I didn't get much attention from colleges. The only schools that offered me a scholarship were Kansas State and Brigham Young University.

I played several positions—quarterback, defensive back, punt/kickoff returner and punter/kicker. In fact, the most nervous I have ever been playing football was while kicking the extra point with the score 99-6 against Kofa High School on Homecoming night. If I'd missed the kick that would have given us 100 points, I never would have gotten over it! Thankfully, I slept soundly that night. And fortunately, I was selected to play in the high school All-Star football game, which was held in Flagstaff in June.

At the All-Star game, I was the starting free safety and the backup quarterback. In the first half, I intercepted three passes. In the second half, I played quarterback and threw three touchdown passes. We won the game 21 to 20. It was definitely a special day for me, likely the best football game I had played to date... and Frank Kush, the Head Football Coach at Arizona State University, was at that game.

Prior to that, ASU had not shown interest in me. But after that game, Coach Kush decided to recruit me. My family had strong ties to ASU, and it was high on my list of schools—sport opportunity or not. My dad and biggest influence was an All-American football player there. And that man was a true alum. He went to every home ASU football game and most of the basketball games. But it was baseball that had my heart.

I had told BYU I was going to accept their scholarship offer and was planning to fly to Utah to sign a letter of intent on a Saturday. The Thursday before, Coach Kush came to our house. He didn't have any more football scholarships to offer, so he got Bobby Winkles, the baseball coach at ASU, on the phone and offered me a baseball scholarship.

A baseball scholarship to ASU in those days was like gold. I decided to turn down BYU, stay at home and accept the ASU baseball scholarship. I knew Dad really wanted me to stay at ASU, but he never said it. That way he could go to all the games, and besides our family bled maroon and gold. My freshman, sophomore, and junior years of college. I played both baseball and football. My sophomore year, the baseball team did really well but lost the College World Series championship game to the University of Southern California. I wanted a second chance.

Best Worst Experience

HJ

His junior year, they made a repeat appearance at the College World Series. They were scheduled to play Minnesota on a Sunday which, if they won, would put them on the road to the National Championship. That was the first time he faced the issue of playing a game on Sunday and he had not forgotten the experience of sitting on the bed with his dad after missing church as a teenager. Growing up in a very strict religious home, he had been taught also by all of his church leaders as a child that if he kept the Sabbath day holy he would be blessed. And he believed it. But this was ASU Baseball.

DW

After praying hard about it, I decided not to play in the game. I had to go tell Coach Brock, the new ASU baseball coach after Coach Winkles left, that I could not play in the game on Sunday for religious reasons. As big as this game was, he couldn't believe I was not going to play, and my teammates would have a hard time understanding. But I followed through and sat in the dugout in my street clothes and watched the game. I had faith I would be blessed.

Thankfully we won, though it was hard for me to watch from the outside. The next day, Monday, we lost to University of Southern California, which put us into the loser's bracket, but a win against Texas on Tuesday set us back up for the championship and the biggest game of my baseball career. The finals were on Wednesday night. In the bottom of the ninth inning, with two outs, we were behind by one run, and I was up to bat. My mind raced as I praised myself for showing discipline and consideration of all the things I had been taught by my parents and church leaders. I knew something profound was about to happen.

Coach Brock came up to me in the on-deck circle and said, "Just look for a pitch you can hit out. That's our best chance."

I knew the best scenario for me was to get ahead in the count and get him to throw me a fastball. I was really good at hitting fastballs, but curveballs...not so much. Sure enough, I got a 2-0 count and knew my fastball was coming next. He couldn't afford to walk me because I was the tying run. He had to throw a strike.

I looked over in the dugout and Coach gave me the "take" sign. I couldn't believe it! Things were going exactly as I hoped and now he wanted me to take the pitch and try to get a walk? The next pitch was exactly what I expected—a fastball waist high and the perfect pitch for me to hit. But I held back. I took it just like my Coach wanted. The next two pitches were curveballs and I struck out.

That was not what was supposed to happen. It was not the "blessing" I expected. I was angry. Angry at my parents. Angry at my church leaders. Angry at everyone who taught me that if I made good decisions I would be blessed. I went to Coach Brock when we got home and told him I was not going to play baseball my senior year. Rather, I was going to concentrate on football.

Not many people know that I struck out to make the final out of the 1973 College World Series and cost ASU the national championship in baseball. It's not a story I share a lot. But, two months later, I was the quarterback on a college football team that was leading the nation in both yardage and points scored. All of a sudden NFL scouts were at all of our practices and games. I was still not a great quarterback, but I was the quarterback on a great team. In my thirty-three games as the starter, we went 30-3 and won the first 3 Fiesta Bowl games.

I was the first quarterback drafted in the 1974 NFL draft by the Dallas Cowboys and I had learned a valuable lesson. God always hears our prayers but sometimes they are not answered in the way or the time that we want or expect, but rather in His time and His way. I believe I was being led in the path that was best for me.

Choosing football over baseball was a great blessing in my life. I am beyond grateful for my church leaders and parents. Sometimes what we want and what's best for us are two different things.

HJ

Closed doors have so much value—sometimes as much as open doors. A closed door narrows the right path by limiting a wrong option.

If I solicited Dad's advice on an important decision,

I could easily bet he would reference Yogi Berra's, "You know what to do when you come to a fork in the road? Take it!" That's how Dad lived his life. Always a risk-taker, he flew to Bogota Colombia for Lasik surgery before it was federally approved in the US. While there, however, his doctor decided a transplant would be better. He ended up having a cornea transplant in a third world country with minimal anesthesia because a donor came available at just the right time. In sports, business, and life in general, risks and failures don't process in his brain the way they do for most people.

When people focus too much on risk, they tend to get stuck, paralyzed even, because fear is activated unproductively. That never happened to Dad. If he failed, he only saw steps. Even if it was a step in the wrong direction, to him it was chalked up to "experience" and a newly gained confidence of which path *not* to take. If you think about it, there was actually tons of value in that.

His example influenced me tremendously. It's an unnatural approach for me, as I think it is for most people. It stems from a certainty that I only ever hope to attain. His faith in God pushed him through the wrong roads and pulled him into the right opportunities all his life.

In his post-NFL years there were plenty of ups and downs, wins and losses. The wins he taught us to accept with dignity and appreciation, the losses with open hands and hearts asking, *what's the lesson here?*

FOOTBALL

ASU

After redirecting focus from baseball to football there were three games that were launching pads for Dad's football career. One was the previously mentioned high school All-Star game in Flagstaff. Another was ASU versus the University of New Mexico his sophomore year. And the third was the Cowboys' playoff game in 1981 versus the Falcons in Atlanta that put Dallas into the championship game. We'll get to that last one later.

During his sophomore year at Arizona State all of the competition disappeared. Several players transferred, and Joe Spagnola, the previous starter, had graduated. It left Dad as one of the backups to Grady Hurst, the new starter. One day at training camp, Coach Kush put Dad in as quarterback with the starting team, just to see how Grady would react. Well…Grady quit. And in a matter of a few months, the soph went from being a defensive back and punter to being the starting quarterback for ASU.

DW

I will never forget the first game I played as the starter. You have to remember, I never dreamed I would even be on the football team let alone be the starting quarterback. It was a home game against the University of Houston, and I was a nervous wreck. Coach Kush could tell.

He came up to me before the game and said, "Hey, White. You look nervous."

I said, "Actually, I am, Coach."

He said, "Aw, don't worry about it. There are eleven players on the field. Ten of them are better runners than you. Just get the ball from the center, hand it to one of them without dropping it, and we'll be fine."

That was his peptalk. We won the game on a last second field goal and we were off to the races. However, in the third game of the year I separated my shoulder. Coach Kush went out and found Grady Hurst again. He brought him back on the team, and my career appeared to be over.

Three weeks later, we lost a game to Oregon State in Corvallis. The following week, we were playing the team we were tied with for the conference lead, the University of New Mexico. It was a huge game. I went with the team to the game in Albuquerque but was in no way ready to play. My shoulder was still recovering, and I couldn't throw very far or with much velocity.

Coach Kush came up to me on the sidelines as the game began and said, "Hey, White, you're starting.

Grady is nervous."

I objected, "Coach, I can hardly throw the ball. I can't start."

His rebuttal? "Aw, don't worry about it, we'll just run the ball."

So I started. On that first series, we ran the ball all the way down the field to about the three-yard line where he called a bootleg pass. I ended up running the play and throwing a short touchdown pass to a wide-open receiver in the end zone.

When I came off the field, Coach said to me, "Hey, White, you're staying in. Grady is still nervous." It was painful just to throw a short pass, now he was going to leave me in the game? The next series started the same way until he called a screen pass. I dropped back and threw the ball about five yards to my tailback, who ran about fifty yards for a touchdown. I played the rest of the game.

At the end of the day, we won the game easily. I was 9/12 for 124 yards and six touchdowns, and I never threw the ball very far. I couldn't. The next day the national press named me the AP and UPI national player of the week. Grady quit again and my football career was back on track. That was a critical and pivotal event in my life, not because of any great effort on my part but because of teammates, coaches, and just plain fate, if that's what you want to call it. The football gods smiled on me, while the baseball gods did not.

I grew up watching a baseball team run by Coach Bobby Winkles and dreamed of playing for him. When he left my freshman year it was the beginning of the end for my baseball career. I loved my baseball teammates and playing the game, but it just wasn't the same without him there. As for my transition from baseball to football, I credit one person. Frank Kush was clearly the reason I became a football player rather than a baseball player. He convinced me that I was tough enough and smart enough to be a quarterback at the college level. He created an environment that a player could thrive in. It was the right system, and I was surrounded with great players to the extent that I could succeed as a quarterback.

My career path went vertical from that point on, and I very quickly realized that it was a lot more exciting to play Quarterback for the ASU football team in front of thousands of fans and on television and radio than it was standing in center field waiting for someone to hit a ball to me. We then went on to win 25 of our next 28 football games. The week following those three losses (one in Laramie, Wyoming, one in Salt Lake City, Utah and one in Tempe, AZ) Frank Kush made it painfully clear that losing was not going to be tolerated as a Sun Devil. We worked harder after a loss than at any other time in the season. Needless to say, we never lost two games in a row. And only once did we lose two games in a season.

HJ

See what I mean about taking risks? This won't be the last reference on that subject, so get comfortable with it. What I love about this story is that someone else was taking the risk on him. Coach Kush rolled the dice on an injured athlete, and it paid off. What he and Dad both gained from it well surpassed the potential loss.

When I was sixteen, my grandpa (Mom's dad) decided he wanted to teach me how to drive a manual vehicle. His definition of teaching wasn't the same as mine, unfortunately. He got out of the car, and we switched seats. "Go ahead. Drive," he said.

I knew nothing at all. "Why are there three pedals?"

48

"You'll figure it out. Just go."

We shouldn't have made it home safely. Actually, I don't think the car was in very good shape when we did, but I'd learned how to drive a manual because someone had enough confidence in me. He'd taken a chance on me, and I jumped in, sustained not by my own confidence but his.

I've adopted dad's approach to risks, and though it doesn't come as naturally, I've tried his attitude toward failure as well. He ingrained those attitudes in his kids. In education, business, and opportunities in general, we tend to advance rather than retreat. Being a risk-taker can give you guts, and I figure that's a good thing. That way, when someone advises you to "go with your gut" at least you've got some.

I took a risk on who I married. We didn't know each other long, nor well. But oh…my guts.

Kelly was not a religious guy growing up, so he was more than surprised when at sixteen years old the local seminary principal found him and asked him to be on the seminary council.

"You're mistaking me for someone else," he replied.

"No I'm not. We want you. We need your kind of people in the seminary."

For whatever reason, Kelly agreed and became the early morning donuts runner for the seminary council. It was risky and unorthodox for that principal to place an irreligious kid as a leader in such an organization. But by doing so, the council lost nothing, and Kelly was set on a path that would lead him to serve a two-year religious mission, which influenced countless lives, ultimately meeting both his business partner and future wife (yep, me) through those associations.

There will be times when we get the opportunity to take a chance on a seemingly unproductive prospect.

What may be of minimal consequence to us, however, may promise huge impact to the prospect. Think about the people who have given you their endorsement, especially those who gave it before you had anything noticeable to offer. These are the people who deserve all the credit. Without them we would still be standing on the sidelines.

Fiesta Bowl, 1971

Coach Kush

HJ
I love this article excerpt I found rummaging through Dad's old boxes...

Kush Lauds Danny's Day

PHOENIX (AP)—Sophomore quarterback Danny White called all his own plays except one, Arizona State University football coach Frank Kush said Monday in describing Saturday's 60-28 romp over New Mexico to the Phoenix Press Box Association.

"That's the first time that a youngster has done that for us," Kush told sportswriters and broadcasters. "Danny probably had the greatest day that a kid can have."

"White completed six scoring passes, setting school and Western Athletic Conference records."

DW

As the Western Athletic Conference champions, ASU played in the first Fiesta Bowl. It was 1971, and we played against Gary Huff and the Florida State Seminoles. Huff was a great quarterback. We battled back and forth, up and down the field like a couple of heavyweight fighters just throwing haymakers. The game came down to whoever had the ball last and luckily, we had it.

From the two-yard line, on a critical third and goal, Coach Kush sent in a pass play. When I called it in the huddle I looked into the faces of Steve Matlock and Roger Davis, the right guard and tackle who looked back at me with mud and blood and sweat streaming down their faces.

Steve said, "No you don't! (I'm cleaning the language up a little here) You run the ball right over us!"

So I changed the play Coach had ordered and called a simple dive play. I gave the ball to Woody Green, and he danced into the endzone for the winning touchdown.

I remember the locker room after the game and how all the reporters gathered around my locker wanting to know how a little sophomore QB had the guts to change a play Frank Kush had called during a critical point of the game.

At the time, I took full credit. "Well, I felt like the run to Woody was a better play against their tired, worn-out defense." I now have to confess…it wasn't me that called that play. It came from Matlock and Davis, who were older and a lot bigger and tougher than me."

HJ

I asked Dad once to tell me what he loved so much about his ASU coach, Frank Kush.

"Oh, I didn't love Coach Kush. In fact, most of the time I didn't even like him."

I couldn't understand. Frank Kush was a household name for us. Someone we heard Dad talk about regularly and positively. At least, to that point, I had never picked up on negativity. Before I could ask for an explanation, Dad followed up.

"He was a phenomenal coach, don't get me wrong. In all honestly, I owe him my career. But there were days I really hated him."

DW

Frank Kush was the toughest man I ever met. He was more responsible for me becoming a football player than anyone else, other than my father. One night we were bussing over to the stadium for a night practice, which we frequently did in order to get used to the lights because most of our games were played at night.

When we got to the stadium, someone had forgotten to unlock the gate to an eight-foot chain link fence that surrounded the stadium. I was sitting next to a window, and I watched as coach Kush got off the bus, went over and checked the lock on the gate, and then slammed his hat down on the ground and stood there, scratching his head, trying to figure out who it was that forgot to open the gate. He walked back over to the bus and stood there for a minute, not knowing what to do. All of a sudden, as if a light went on in his head, he jumped up in the bus, pulled the driver out of his seat and pushed him off the bus. He got behind the wheel and drove the bus right through the gate, breaking the chain that was holding it together. No way a coach could get away with something like that today.

On another occasion, we were again at the stadium practicing at night. We had just left Camp Tontozona, which is in the mountains north of Tempe where we went for a couple of weeks to practice in the summer prior to our season starting. Coach Kush had told us the day we left camp that we were going back to the valley to get some rest before our first game, so he was going to go easy on our practices. He said he wanted us to try to "get some of the spring back in our legs" because we had worked extremely hard at camp.

That first night after our "easy" practice, he was upset with the way that we practiced. So, he lined us up on the goal line and ran "grass drills" all the way down the field and back. A grass drill is a five-yard drill where you start at the goal line and run to the five-yard line, then run back to the goal-line, then back to the five, back to the goal-line, touching the line at each turn, then you run through the five on the last run. So five turns, five lines touched, twenty-five yards ran. That was one drill. We would repeat this on each ten-yard line all the way down the field, constituting ten grass drills. We were all standing at the end of the field, expecting to get on the bus to go back to the locker room when he lined us up again to do another round.

One of our defensive linemen, Deke Ballard, said mostly under his breath, "Yeah this is sure getting the spring back in our legs."

Coach Kush heard him. He turned around and yelled, "Who said that?" Nobody said a word, so Coach Kush said, "Okay, we're gonna run grass drills until I find out who said that."

We were lining up to run again when Deke yelled out, "I said it, Coach."

"Okay, Ballard get on the line," Kush said. He blew his whistle and Deke ran a grass drill all by himself. He blew the whistle again and ran another one. He blew it again, and Deke ran another one. By now, in total exhaustion, Deke laid on the ground, his chest heaving, trying to catch his breath. Coach Kush walked over to him and standing over him, said, "Well maybe that'll get some of the spring out of your lips."

I could go on and on with stories about Frank Kush. The one thing I will say about him is that he got the very most out of those of us who stayed with him. I say that because over half of the players who started out in the ASU program in those days ended up leaving because they couldn't put up with Frank Kush. I owe my entire career to him because I never dreamed I would be a football player. He surrounded me with the kind of players I needed in order to be successful. He is the one who made it possible for a skinny baseball player from Mesa, Arizona to have a thirteen-year career in the NFL.

Stadium Lights

HJ

It's worth mentioning here that the spotlights in Texas Stadium burned a little hotter and brighter than most stadiums in those golden years. The Cowboys weren't just under a spotlight, they were under a high-powered microscope under a spotlight. Everything that could be analyzed was analyzed, from stats to cheerleaders to traveling attire, to players' home life...to the color of jerseys.

DW

Game day was the highlight of my career. To step onto an NFL field, especially in Texas Stadium, wearing a helmet with the iconic blue star on both sides was pretty special.

Back then, game-day prep wasn't as big a deal as it is today. Early in my career, if it was a home game, I simply spent the night before the game at home, woke up and drove to the stadium. Later in my career, we started spending the night before a game in a hotel in the Dallas area. We still drove our own vehicles to the stadium and got there as early as we wanted. Everybody was different. Some guys wanted to get there early, but I didn't like having a lot of extra time in the locker room. I would just get to the stadium in time for our quarterback meeting. Then I would don that white cowboy uniform with my blue number eleven and hit the field for warm-ups.

We always wore our white jerseys for home games. Since the home team got to choose whether they wore light or dark colored jerseys, we always chose white at home. This was contrary to every other team in the league—a decision born from a phobia against wearing our blue jerseys. The fans seemed to think it was bad luck because our win/loss record was worse in blue than white. So since all the other teams wore their colored jerseys at home, we wore white jerseys for almost every game.

That was one of the little things that gave us a slight advantage. On our offensive practice day (Wednesday), we would wear white jerseys for practice and the defense would wear blue. Then, we would switch on Thursday. That way if we saw white in the corner of our eye in a game, we knew it was a teammate. This was especially helpful to quarterbacks trying to see the defensive coverage and picking out open receivers.

Unpredictability is one of the great things about the game of football. Every play is a touchdown when you draw it up on paper. But each play is a new experience, and rarely does it happen in reality the way it's designed to happen. And there are countless contributing factors, including a bunch of guys on the other side of the ball that are pretty good football players also.

Technically speaking, every play that doesn't result in a touchdown is a failure. So, as a football player, you have to get used to dealing with failure. You have to get over it very quickly and move on to the next play, or the next series, or the next game, or the next season.

As a Dallas Cowboy, if you didn't win the Super Bowl, the season was considered a failure by the fans and the media. It was clearly not the organization to be a part of if you were content with mediocrity.

HJ

From a young age I was trained to focus on how others

perceived me. It was one of the curses of growing up under the microscope, and it became a fixation. Worrying about what others thought became an obsession to the point where I felt my very safety and the safety of my family was in jeopardy if I misbehaved.

It took time to reroute that path in my brain and to understand that part of being self-sufficient was to free yourself from the bondage of others' judgements.

Recently, my daughter asked me to help her pick out an outfit. I was busy and took too long to give her my full attention, so by the time I was ready to help her, she'd made her decision.

"Your opinion is no longer valid," she informed me.

I'm sure she meant it as a dig, but I only felt proud. As soon as you make a decision, others' opinions should become irrelevant. Most often you're wrong about what they're thinking anyway.

People would ask me and the boys, tongue-in-cheek, what our daddy did for a living. They already knew the answer. I guess they just craved the rarity, but we wouldn't take the bait. We would say stuff like, "He mows our lawn" or "He takes me fishing." We weren't being intentionally insolent. Funny enough, those were our honest feelings. So he played some football games. He did a lot of things when we weren't with him, but who cared about those? Too often we put more emphasis on what we do rather than who we are, and that should be reversed.

Still young kids, my brothers and I didn't go to many games, definitely not as often as my brothers wanted. They loved the games, especially Ryan. For me, the stadium was smokey and noisy, and those game nights felt endless. Staying home was much better. I'm sure the game was on the TV, but I didn't always care to watch. Except for once. Dad had broken his wrist, and I colored a big flower on his cast with markers. I wanted so badly to see my flower on the TV!

Mom said she only ever missed two of Dad's home games. One was the day after I was born, and they put a message up on the jumbotron announcing my arrival.

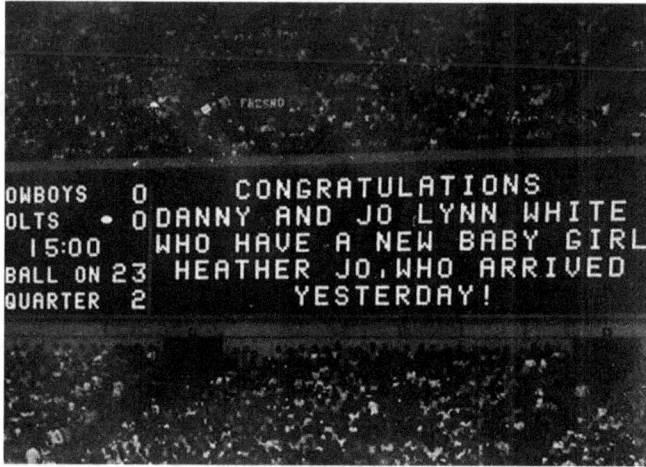

That game was the regular season opener and Dallas beat Baltimore 38-0. That season the Cowboys were 12 and 4 and beat LA in the NFC Division Championship Game, 28-0. Boom. Good year to be born.

As an adult, I've come around. I love the game and cheer with the die-hards. But in those formative years it just wasn't on my radar unless my art was on display. If someone asked me who I was rooting for, I knew I was obligated to give an informed response, so I would glance at the teams and choose which color jersey I liked better. Apparently, jersey colors mattered in ways I was totally oblivious to. I wonder how many other things mattered.

The Dallas Cowboys

DW

Gameday was the climax of the week. It was the reward for all the hard work and preparation...as long as we won. Losing was awful. It was as if the whole week was wasted, and we might as well have not even shown up for the game. Especially on the road with all the packing and checking in at the hotel and the plane trip. We might as well have just stayed home and relaxed with the family rather than go through all that just to lose a football game.

As a Dallas Cowboy, winning was expected — losing was not. I came from a winning culture at ASU, but it was nothing compared to the culture I was about to enter in Dallas.

For the first four years of my career, I was the backup quarterback to Roger Staubach, and was also the punter. That was a real benefit, because I had four years to get used to that culture. I grew comfortable with the routine, taking the field for pregame warm-ups and then once again for the start of the game.

I became the starter in 1980 after Roger retired. Once I was introduced as the starting quarterback and I took the field for that first snap, my life changed dramatically. The pressure placed on me intensified. I remember the relief I felt every game after that first play, and especially after the first time I got hit. It knocked the cobwebs out of me and instantly gave me confidence. All the work, all the preparation was finally paying off. Now I could just settle down and play the game. Now it was fun. Now I was doing something very few people ever get to do.

I got to play quarterback...in the NFL...for the Dallas Cowboys...America's Team.

There were times when, looking back, I questioned whether things that happened to me, happened simply as a result of chance. Were the football gods smiling on me? Or was I somehow being guided by a higher power? Was my life and career actually being directed?

In my first year as a starter, our record was 12-4 and we made the playoffs. We were playing the Atlanta Falcons in Atlanta, and the winner would go on to the NFC championship game in Philadelphia. It was brutally cold in Atlanta that day. We had done very little offensively throughout the game. With four minutes to go, we were trailing by 10 points, 27 to 17.

We started throwing the ball more, trying to catch up. On one play, I scrambled to my right and threw a pass to Drew Pearson in the end zone for a touchdown. I remember seeing that number 88 and pointing for him to go to his left. Then I watched the defenders (who were also watching me) move to where I was pointing while Drew just stayed where he was. Suddenly he was wide open, standing in the right corner of the end zone all alone. At least, that's what I thought I saw. When we watched the film the next day, I was shocked to see five Falcon defenders in the picture with Drew. Five! He was not only covered. Or double covered. Or triple covered. He was quintuple covered. He just outjumped everyone for the ball and came down with it for a touchdown. *Teammates.* It was now 27 to 24, with three minutes to go in the game. The defense stopped them, and we got the ball back with under a minute to go. We worked the ball down to the twenty-yard line and were sitting comfortably in field goal position and down three points. This is where, as a quarterback, you have to play smart. A turnover at this point would be disastrous. We called timeout and I went to the sideline and talked to Coach Landry about our next play. As I ran out onto the field Coach Landry yelled at me, "Danny, don't do anything stupid!" I knew exactly what he meant.

I went right out there and made what may have been the stupidest decision of my career. We had a pass play called. Preston Pearson was behind me in the backfield and on the snap of the ball, he went to his left when he was supposed to go to his right. The linebacker to my right blitzed and it didn't look like he was going to be blocked, so I threw the ball hot (quickly) to avoid getting sacked. A sack there would put us further away from the goal posts and a successful field goal and overtime. I had to get rid of the ball and avoid a sack. I threw it right into traffic. With a field goal in the bag, it was the last thing a quarterback should do. That's what pressure (a blitzing linebacker) can do to a quarterback—force him to make a bad decision.

Preston, after going to his left, came back to the right and blocked the blitzer. As it turned out, I didn't have to throw the ball hot. It was a terribly risky throw. With only 42 seconds left we could have tied it up easily and headed into overtime.

Fortunately, and for no real logical reason, Drew looked back for the ball. The ball got to him just as he looked back, and right at the goal line. It was as if he sensed the ball was coming to him. I believe great players who consistently make great plays have an enhanced sensory system, almost animalistic. He made the catch for a touchdown and the win. Had it been anyone else or had the Falcons safety gotten there a split second sooner, it would've been an interception—disastrous for the team and for me and my career. I wouldn't have been able to show my face in Dallas. That ball should never have been thrown. *Teammates.*

After the touchdown, two of my favorite teammates, tight end Jay Saldi and receiver Butch Johnson were jumping on top of me on the sideline yelling "Roger who? Roger who?" The media and fans were proclaiming that I had exorcized the ghost of Roger Staubach from our closet. This was my "Hail Mary." A stupid throw that could've gone wrong in so many ways. That's another thing about the game of football. The greatest plays in the history of the game didn't happen by design. The "Hail Mary". The "Immaculate Reception". The "Catch". Great players will tell you, if they're honest, that there were a lot of times when they just got lucky. It's just that great players seem to get lucky more than most. Someone once said, "Luck is what happens when preparation meets opportunity". Anyway, we were headed to Philadelphia and the NFC Championship game.

I've had countless near-misses and just as many near-wins. There was another game against Miami when I threw a ball to Ron Springs and had a similar result. I never should've thrown the ball, but somehow it worked out for us.

Sometimes we do all the right things but get the wrong results. And sometimes we do all the wrong things and end up with the right results. We have a lot less control over our circumstances than we realize. All we can really control is how we react to those results.

"The Tackle"

Another event that could very possibly have put me on the top rung of the ladder as a football player was the 1981 championship game against the San Francisco 49ers. Most people recognize this game as "The Catch" game but I refer to it as "The Tackle" game because as big a play as the catch was, the tackle of Drew Pearson by Eric Wright on the next to last play of the game to me was even bigger.

Once again, we were playing the championship game in enemy territory and not in the friendly confines of Texas Stadium. This became a real plague for us. All three championship games in the first three years of my career as a starter were played on the road and not at home. Texas Stadium had become a real advantage for us. We won eighteen games in a row at Texas Stadium–six at the end of Roger's career and twelve at the beginning of mine–an NFL record we still hold to this day.

The score of the game went back-and-forth for fifty-six minutes. I felt really good about the outcome after punting the ball down to the 11-yard line forcing the 49ers to go 89 yards against our defense and needing to score a touchdown with the score 26 to 21 in our favor. But managing the clock brilliantly, Joe Montana and Coach Bill Walsh moved the ball all the way down the field and scored on "The Catch" to Dwight Clark with just fifty-one seconds left in the game.

After the kickoff we had just forty-five seconds left in the game to go the entire field with the score now 28 to 27 for the 49ers. In those next forty-five seconds I probably had the best and worst plays of my career. In the huddle, on the first play, we called a Red Left, Lee 16. This is a play that calls for Drew Pearson to run a 15-yard crossing route. In the huddle I told Drew to go 20 yards instead of 15. I knew they were going to be playing a very soft defense and I wanted to be able to get the ball over the linebackers and underneath the defensive safeties. This adjustment proved to be critical to the success of the play and almost won the game for us.

I remember thinking as I got the ball and dropped back that I needed to hold the safety in place by looking to the right, and then coming back at the last second to the left and throwing the ball into the hole between the linebackers and the safeties, hoping that Drew would time the route appropriately based on the extra yardage.

He did just that. He timed it perfectly and as the ball came down at the 20-yard mark, he came into the hole just as the ball got there. He caught the ball in full stride, and I thought he was headed for the endzone with another miracle finish similar to the Hail Mary. But just as he turned up field, Eric Wright grabbed him by the back of his shoulder pads and pulled him down from behind, preventing what might have been a touchdown, but would have at least gained extra yardage getting us closer to field goal range.

If that play happened with today's rules, it would have been penalized as a horse collar tackle, resulting in a penalty of 15 yards and putting us into field goal range for a go-ahead field goal. But that rule didn't exist back then and so we had about another 10 yards to go in order to be close enough for Rafael Septien to kick a field goal.

Coach Landry then called a pass play to Tony Dorsett. It was a play that I did not have a lot of confidence in and in hindsight I wish I had called a different play. But the decision had to be made, as so many in the game of football are, in a matter of a few seconds. I chose to stick with the play called and try to pick up the 10 or 15 yards necessary to kick a field goal and win the game.

As I dropped back to pass, I set up and started to throw the ball to Tony. When I saw the defensive back starting to close on him and halfway through my motion, I pulled the ball down, choosing to find another receiver or run with the ball. Again, in hindsight, I wish I had just rolled out of the pocket and taken off with it, but I was concerned about losing yardage and getting sacked, which would've knocked us farther back and out of field goal range. The 49ers ran a stunt with their pass rush up the middle that got pressure on me very quickly. Before

I could get both hands on the ball they hit me, knocking the ball out of my hands. They recovered the fumble which ended any possibility of us scoring and winning the game.

So instead of winning the game and heading to the Super Bowl against the Cincinnati Bengals, our season was over. All the work. All the study and preparation. All the sacrifices of an entire year ended in a matter of seconds. In the blink of an eye.

So often in the game of football, history is written based on the results of fluke plays and not necessarily by design. The "Hail Mary", the "Immaculate Reception", and "The Catch" are just three examples of some of the greatest plays in the history of the NFL that were mostly a matter of great players being in the right place at the right time and not really the way the plays were supposed to happen. We ended up getting back to the championship game the following year, losing once again to the Washington Redskins. The 49ers went on to win four Super Bowls and become the team of the 80s in the NFL.

Such is the life of an NFL quarterback. Split second decisions can result in historical events because the thing that separates a quarterback from every other position in football is decision-making. Most other players simply execute their assignments, but quarterbacks have to make decisions. In my opinion, decision-making is what separates the great quarterbacks from all the others. On any pass play, a quarterback has as many as five or six options to choose from and usually has two to four seconds to make those decisions. Do I throw it? Do I run with it? Do I throw it away? Do I take a sack? All of these can be the right decision on any given play. This is what makes the quarterback position the most important position of any team sport in the world. Quarterbacks who have strong arms and are good runners are a dime a dozen. But quarterbacks who can make good, quick decisions, and do it consistently even while under great pressure either physically or mentally, are rare.

"Tony Dorsett into history"

I've always believed that in order to achieve greatness you must first be in a position to achieve greatness. Like the Phoenix bird rising out of the ashes, first it had to be in ashes. The Arizona State University football team in 2024 was picked to finish dead last in the Big 12 Conference, which is comprised of 16 teams. Well, not only did they not finish last, this band of rejects ended up winning the conference championship.

I say "band of rejects" because most of the players came to ASU through the NCAA portal after not being wanted by the schools they were currently at. ASU head coach, Kenny Dillingham, the youngest head coach in Division 1 football and only in his second year as a head coach, did a masterful job of bringing together a group of young men who created synergy in the locker room. Their chemistry off and on the field helped them overcome adversity after adversity and challenge after challenge. Against Iowa State, they won 45 to 19 in a game they were not even supposed to win let alone dominate to win the Big 12 Championship. This was an accomplishment that will probably never happen again, mostly because ASU will probably never again be picked to finish last in the conference, at least not for a very, very long time.

Part of what makes this a great example of achieving greatness is the fact that expectations were so low, picked by all the experts to finish last. I was privileged to be a very small part of this team as a staff consultant to Coach Dillingham, which means I was able to hang out with the players, on and off the field, travel with them to all the games, and be on the sideline. I watched the power of that synergy at its very best. This validated something I've always believed, which is that cohesion and camaraderie is just as important as talent in the game of football, the greatest of all team sports.

Another example of greatness that will never be matched, and that I had a small part to play in was Tony Dorsett's 99+ yard run in the NFL. Tony was one of my all-time favorite teammates. When he joined us on the Cowboys team in 1977, we were already a good team. The Cowboys won the Super Bowl in 1972, then in 1976 (my rookie year after 2 years in Memphis in the WFL) we were upset 14-12 by the Rams in the Divisional playoff game. In the '77 draft we grabbed Tony Dorsett in the first round. He almost single-handedly took us from good to great, and we beat Denver in the 1978 Super Bowl. Then, in a game in 1982 in the new Minneapolis Metrodome, after throwing a pick-six and going even further behind the Vikings and drawing the wrath and verbal thrashing of one Howard Cosell, who most football fans will remember as one of the major critics of the game of football in the '60s and '70s, history was about to be made. And not just any ordinary history, but history that will never be broken. Unless, that is, they lengthen the field to over 100 yards.

After the Vikings scored, they kicked off to us and Timmy Newsome mishandled the kickoff, ending up pushing the ball out of bounds at the half yard line. Cosell then commented to a national TV audience that he had never seen the Cowboys look worse and that it appeared to him we believed we could just snap our fingers and turn a game around. Well, what happened next was just as he had facetiously predicted. We talked briefly on the sideline about what to do and Coach Landry gave me a play to run. I ran out on the field, got in the huddle, and called the play. As we broke to the line of scrimmage, I saw our fullback, Ron Springs, run off the field for some unknown reason, leaving us with only ten players on the field.

As the play clock ticked below ten seconds, I had a decision to make. Do I use one of our valuable timeouts? (In a game where we were behind and would need all those timeouts in order to win.) Or do I go ahead and run the play with only ten players on the field, risking a safety and falling another two points behind, in addition to giving the ball back to the Vikings? As the clock approached zero, I went ahead and ran the play. The result of that decision was an entry into the history books of the NFL that will never be erased. The back end of the football was literally on the goal line when we snapped the ball. Tony broke through the line of scrimmage and with an incredible block down field from Drew Pearson, the guy that made more big plays in big games than anyone that I know. (A deserving Hall of Famer who made some great catches in his career, including the Hail Mary from Roger Staubach against these same Minnesota Vikings.) Tony Dorsett went from end zone to end zone, giving us the victory. In my opinion, Drew's block on that play may have been the greatest of his career. I like to feel that I also played a role in that event by running the play rather than calling timeout. This was a decision that, as a quarterback, I could have been severely criticized for had it resulted in a safety.

The point I'm trying to make in all of this is that like the Phoenix bird, or the ASU Football team or Tony Dorsett's record-breaking run, none of these great achievements would have been as great had it not been for an almost hopeless starting point. We all need to remember that when all hope has fled and we feel like we have no chance at all, we should never quit. Because under the right conditions and with the right people round us, nothing is ever truly impossible. In fact, only then are we in position to achieve greatness.

"Heros"

As I was growing up in grade school and high school I had sports heroes like everybody else. In football it was Bart Starr, the quarterback of the Green Bay Packers. In basketball it was Jerry West and the Los Angeles Lakers. And in baseball it was Mickey Mantle and the whole New York Yankees baseball team. Every one of them was great on the field or court, but it was off the court or field that made me idolize them the most. They were all good examples of how I thought a professional athlete should handle themselves with the standards I had learned from my dad. I wanted to grow up to be one of those heroes to young men everywhere.

Once I got to the point of celebrity, though, I realized what a hard thing it was to be that guy all the time to everyone, because wherever I went I was recognized. And sometimes people could be very rude in the way they approached me so I got to the point where I wouldn't go out in public. But if I did, I would wear some sort of disguise, like a hat with sunglasses, so as not to be recognized. I didn't want to be confronted by obnoxious Dallas Cowboys fans who would ask the same old stupid questions like, " What is it like playing for Coach Landry?" or "What's it like playing in the Super Bowl?" I didn't want to be rude and just walk away but most of the time I was in a hurry to get somewhere, so I tried to just avoid them.

My greatest fear was getting trapped on an airplane seated next to one of those obnoxious fans who was going to ask those same questions over and over and over for the length of the flight, and I had no way to escape. I would board planes and immediately put up a newspaper or a magazine in front of my face so as not to be recognized.

One day while flying from Dallas to Atlanta, I did just that. Sure enough a gentleman got on and was heading to the seat next to me. He put his bag in the overhead and then sat down. I hid the newspaper up over my face for almost the entire two hour flight. Just as we were descending into Atlanta, he got up to put his bag back in the overhead. I instantly recognized him as the former quarterback of the Green Bay Packers, Bart Starr! When he sat again, I immediately went into worship mode. I introduced myself and asked him, "What was it like playing for Vince Lombardi?" and "What was it like playing in the Ice Bowl?" I had been seated next to my childhood hero for two hours and didn't even know it. I did get a signed picture from Bart so the trip wasn't completely wasted.

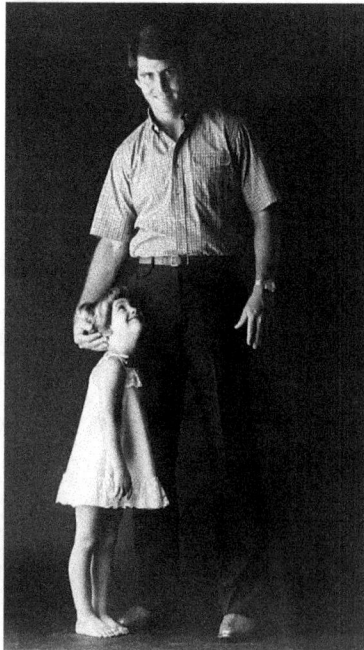

HJ

When people would ask me what it was like having a famous father, it irritated me a little, but not because they were too pushy or inquisitive. It bothered me because they weren't seeing the real guy. We didn't sit around the kitchen table polishing his Super Bowl ring, we just ate pancakes. He didn't sign footballs for us, he signed permission slips for us. He took us camping and taught us how to fish. He was a great dad not because of what he did for work, but because he chose to be a stand-up father.

I don't know if it's his nature or his experience, but I cannot remember a time my dad has ever lost his temper. He is nearly impossible to provoke. I have been with him many times when an outburst would have been expected, even warranted, and his reaction is cool and collected. A simple "Dad gum" or "Shoot" is the most we ever got.

If you asked my kids what my single most frequent *momism* is, they would all say, "You control you!" With gusto, I hope. When a driver cuts you off on the road, he's not making you upset. You let yourself get upset. When a message notification pings on your phone, does your phone control you? Or do you control you? This topic of control has been around for a long time. From ancient Stoic philosophers to contemporary experts, the consensus is that focusing on areas we can control leads to resilience, less stress and anxiety, and more positive emotions and wellbeing.

I have a daughter who is overcoming some severe health problems. We lost track a long time ago of emergency visits and hospital admissions. It's frustrating when we feel like we're doing all the right things to treat and manage her illness and still she backslides. A handful of times we've been with her in the hospital with absolutely no ability to influence whether or not she pulls through. Those are the worst days. In those moments I have to hone in on the things I can control. Worrying about what's out of my hands has zero benefit.

Frustration often comes because we're either:

- Trying to control something/someone we can't
- Letting something/someone else control us

Have you ever sent an email to the wrong recipient? Used grass killer instead of fertilizer, or put a red sock in the white wash? While running late for an appointment, have you ever taken a shortcut only to end up behind an active-duty school bus?

In many situations, there's nothing you can do to remediate. All you can do is deal. It may seem like your control is gone, but that's far from true and probably when your decisions have the most significant consequences. Your attitude and choices when you're in a bind are the most revealing of character. "You control you" in these critical times, and with that attitude you'll be able to turn losses into wins. Learn a new route, check labels, offer apologies. Those are wins.

It's natural for a child to think their father is the toughest man in the world, and I was no exception. Dad often came home pretty beat up. I didn't like that part of the job. Stitches and bruises were the regular part of the "Daddy's home" scene, but he would always laugh it off.

This taught me a lot about progress. Discomfort is necessary for growth. Fear and uncertainty are part of the process. They're mountains between you and your success, and you can't go around them. You have to get over them.

Sometimes we can go back and fix mistakes. Other times, the best we can do is embrace ownership of our actions and reactions. I'm so thankful to Dad for instilling this understanding. I use it both professionally and personally every day. There's not a lot you can do about the weather, your kids' tempers, delayed flights, bad haircuts, or a gazillion other things, but you can control you. Don't give that power to anyone or anything else.

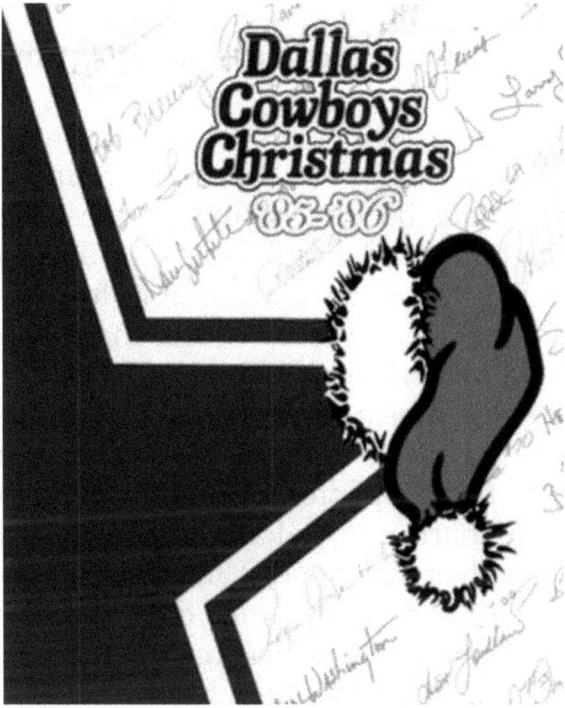

Benefits

DW

Music has always been very important to me. In 1986 and '87 Chris Christian and I had an idea to make a Christmas video by bringing several of my teammates, and even Coach Landry into a studio to sing a bunch of Christmas songs he wrote and make a Christmas video, something the Chicago Bears did the year before. Chris is one of the most talented people I know and has become a good friend.

That may have been the most fun I had in my years in Dallas, outside of playing football. Seeing these guys, who all thought they could sing, go into a studio, and actually perform on a screen was a blast. The raw footage of those videos with the guys trying to get the words and the music together is one of my most priceless possessions.

Convincing Coach Landry to perform to "The Twelve Days of Christmas" — actually, getting him into a studio at all — was maybe one of my greatest achievements during my time in Dallas. Besides the sheer uniqueness of the video, the fact we were able to donate a lot of money to some very worthy causes made it very special. I'm grateful to Chris for all his hard work.

Once again, music played a role in my life. That video was a way for me to combine two of my real passions, music and football, into something of value, to raise money for charity. A collateral benefit was bringing players together. Doing stuff like that off the field as a team created a bond that carried over to the field. At least it did back then. I'm not sure that personal relationships are as important in the game today as they were then. For me, having confidence in the people around me, not just as football players, but also as "brothers in arms" was a very important part of being successful.

Walter Payton on drums. Me on keyboard.

Left to right, Vince Ferragamo, Brenda Lee,
Barbara Mandrell, Steve Gatlin, Rudy Gatlin,
Terry Bradshaw, Me.

Left to right, Vince Ferragamo, Gladys Knight, Brenda Lee, Barbara Mandrell, and Me. Walter Payton is behind Barbara playing drums.

Reed with a very young Garth Brooks and a friend.

One of my all-time favorites Barbara Mandrell.

After his show in Vegas, my alter-ego in music
Kenny Rogers.

Presenting George Straight his first
Platinum Award

Landry

DW

In my opinion, one of the things that made Tom Landry exceptional was his attention to detail. There were so many little factors he could see that other teams gave no attention to. The Cowboys' players weren't bigger, stronger, or faster. We just had these little things that gave us not only an edge in the game but inflated our confidence because we knew we were the only ones doing it.

One example was the jerseys. Another was the flex

defense where the alignment of the tackle and the end gave us a one-step advantage.

On the offensive side, we rigorously practiced a rhythmic cadence on our snap count which, when implemented properly, gave us another slight advantage. By perfecting that cadence we could anticipate the snap rather than respond to it, like other teams had to do. We also had the offensive line and running backs shift before each snap. It not only confused the defense, it blocked their view. There are teams today that greatly magnify that concept, the Dolphins, the Chiefs, and the Cowboys are the best at it. It forces the defense to communicate very quickly as they change coverages with every motion. One breakdown in communication will result in a wide-open receiver running down the field for a touchdown. It takes time to practice these things and that's why more teams don't do more of it. I really feel that the limits in practice time that have been implemented by the Players Association has really hurt the game. Not only creatively, but also physically as I believe there are more injuries, as a result of players, just simply not spending as much time hitting on the practice field as we did.

We were the only team that did these things and it's all because of Coach Landry's impeccable attention to detail. It took a lot of time in practice and in the meeting room to perfect them, but we were willing to take that time.

There's one other Landry-ism I have to mention because, in retrospect, it was one of the real highlights of game week for me. That was the Saturday night (the night before the game) phone call. He would spend the day before the game watching film and would always have some last-minute changes to the game plan that he wanted to review with me.

The phone would ring (those were the days of

actual land lines). There would be no chit-chat or even introductions, just the very recognizable voice of Coach Landry talking, almost in mid-sentence, about a play or situation that might occur in the game the next day. He would say something like, "If we have a slant 36 called and they play a Frisco stack defense, we need to get out of it and go to slant 37." He would then re-emphasize the importance of using our audible system (changing the play at the line of scrimmage using a live color and number) to get out of a bad play once we saw the defense line up.

He was intent on us only using the audible reactively and not opportunistically. The next chapter includes a great example of why. Basically, he didn't want me to be greedy and try to get into a better play.

This was the essence of the Saturday night phone call. These were things that I needed to commit to memory by gametime the next day.

Having the ability to memorize things very quickly was a huge benefit in Coach Landry's system. I trained my brain by memorizing poetry whenever I had time. We would get the weekly game plan on Tuesday night and needed to have it mostly memorized by Wednesday's practice. We had literally hundreds of plays in our playbook, and each play could be run from multiple formations. Coach would not run a play one week from the same formation that we ran it from in the previous week, because that gave the opposing defensive coaches a way to prepare for us. Therefore, each play and its formations would change from week to week.

Back then, the coaches didn't have the ability to talk to their quarterback between plays on the field like they do now through a microphone and a receiver in the quarterback's helmet. So we used a signaling system where the backup quarterback and/or an assistant coach (one being "live" and the other being "fake" to keep the other team from picking up our signals) would signal the play to the quarterback on the field. That meant it was important to be able to memorize signals, plays, and formations very quickly, sometimes even during the course of a game.

Fortunately, it came easy to me. I memorized poems like The Race, Casey at the Bat, The Little Red Hen, and many others to develop my memorizing skills. Once again, taking piano lessons in my youth and learning to memorize songs became a very useful talent as a quarterback in the NFL.

In today's game, it's not nearly as important because the play caller simply tells the quarterback what he wants him to know by talking to him. But for me, the Saturday night phone call was an important part of the process so that we could be on the same page during the game.

I never knew if the call would last two minutes or thirty, but it was Coach Landry talking and me taking notes until he would simply hang up the phone. There was no, "See you tomorrow" or "Have a good night." Just a dial tone when he was done talking. Gameday had begun, and he was all business, or as he called it, "bidness."

Coach Landry had started doing this during Roger's career, and so, to my knowledge, Roger and I were the only two players that had the pleasure of receiving that Saturday night phone call.

HJ

If you're going to be scrutinized under an intense microscope, it's beneficial to have someone that checks every box twice. Tom Landry was that guy for the

Dallas Cowboys, and he shared a huge responsibility in accomplishing their success.

I wonder how many times one of us kids answered the phone for that Saturday night phone call with Coach. With multiple phones in the house all tapping into the same landline it's probable they had some interruptions.

Anyone who's worked with a team knows that regular collaboration is imperative to achievement. But one thing that set Coach Landry apart was his belief that aptitude was less important than alignment. As you'll see in his "key to success", he was more concerned with shared focus than sheer talent. Those weekly calls kept the Cowboys' level of leadership at peak performance.

I don't remember anything special about Saturday nights. I do remember, however, Monday nights. Those were "family nights", and they were a high priority. We rotated weekly assignments that included a game selection, lesson, treats, prayers, etc.

Family Night wasn't always successful or productive. I remember one time mom thought it would be fun to open the popcorn popper while we gathered close to have popcorn bursting all around us like confetti. The only problem was, we had an electric stirring hot oil popper. Don't try that at home, kids. Lots of screaming and tears that night. Another time, we had a lesson on kindness and each of us was given a rubber band to wear on our wrist. The intent was for us to snap ourselves with the rubber band each time we caught ourselves being unkind. Well, unfortunately we were more attentive to when a sibling was unkind and took liberties with *their* bands. Again, tears and screaming as that got out of hand quickly.

Failures and trauma aside, Family Night was something to be counted on. It was a seemingly insignificant ritual but kept our connection to each other strong. The lessons given were ancillary to the fact that we were fully committed to each other and making time once a week to gather and focus on family.

In goal setting, the most critical factors are often the smallest ones — the little details you implement as actions to push you toward your goal. A plan or vision of the big picture is vital, sure, but without the small steps, that plan will crumble. Let your vision be far enough ahead that you're clear on the direction, but not so far that you lose sight of your feet. Like Coach Landry, pay close attention to the details at hand. Because the very next step you take is the most important, no matter how small it seems.

No Danny No!!

DW
Roger and I enjoyed another privilege together that I don't believe any other players were privy to. That was the "brook trout" look (named by Roger). It was a combination of a side-eye glance and a rolled eye from Coach after we did something stupid. Roger got it occasionally. I got it a lot. To my knowledge, no one else had the audacity to buck him like we did.

Our stupid moves had two potential outcomes. If what we did didn't work, we got a lecture. But if it worked, then we got the brook trout look. It was Landry's way of sending the message, 'You got away with it that time, but you better not do it again.' I got it every time I ran with the ball from punt formation instead of kicking it. Every time I did it, it was a huge benefit to the team so he could never say too much.

Except for the first time I faked a punt. It was my rookie year against the Steelers. During the fourth quarter, we really struggled on offense. I was backing up Roger, so I felt extremely frustrated not being able to do anything about it. So the next time we punted, I got in the huddle and called a fake punt that we had practiced. That was the difference. It was premeditated. The play was a failure, and so I, being just a rookie at the time, ran over to the bench and put a jacket over myself trying to hide from the inevitable lecture from Coach Landry. It didn't work.

I was looking down at the ground when I saw two dress shoes walk up in front of me. There was only one person in the stadium that day in Pittsburg wearing dress shoes. I looked up into the eyes of Coach Landry. Staring down at me from underneath that famous fedora, he shook his head and said in his South Texas drawl, "Ya cayn't do it! Ya just cayn't do it!" That was it. Never another word. I wanted him to punch me or kick me or fine me, but none of that. I think deep down he appreciated the fact that I hated losing and wanted to contribute somehow. After that, all my fake punts were impromptu. I would catch the ball, check the rush and then decide if I'd run with it or kick it, or run then kick. Never called in the huddle. Never premeditated. And they always worked — equivalent of a turnover. That also helped.

When I joined the Dallas Cowboys, my rookie year, I was introduced to quarterback school. This was a three-day event held by Coach Landry and included offensive and defensive quarterbacks. The offensive quarterbacks obviously were the quarterbacks. The defensive quarter-backs were the middle linebackers and weak and strong safeties.

On the first day of quarterback school, I got there early and sat on the very front row trying hard to impress not only Coach Landry but also my teammates. He walked into the room and, without welcoming anybody, simply said, "What is the most important thing to know in a football game? Is it *what* to do, *when* to do it, or *why* you do it?" Without much delay my hand just shot up. I immediately heard giggling behind me coming from Roger Staubach, Charlie Waters, and Cliff Harris. Coach Landry looked at me rather puzzled and said, "What is it, Dan?"

I didn't realize that it was a rhetorical question. I thought he wanted an answer, so I raised my hand. All the others had been through quarterback school before. They knew he was about to give us the answer and didn't really want any comments. But he accepted my enthusiasm as I blurted out, "Coach, I have the answer."

"Well, what is it, Dan?"

"Well, if you know *why* you do something then you automatically know *what* to do and *when* to do it. Therefore, the most important thing to know in a football game is *why* you do something."

He seemed a little shocked and then came back with, *"That's very impressive for a rookie... but it's wrong. The most important thing to know in a football game is* **when** *to do something."*

He then continued on with quarterback school without even discussing the question. That really bothered me, but I thought I better leave well enough alone, so I didn't say anything. He asked this question every year at the start of quarterback school, but I refused to comment, not wanting to add insult to injury.

When I became the starting quarterback, I got a little braver and began to answer the question as I had before. Knowing *why* you do something is the most important thing in a football game. He continued to disagree, and I just figured we were just gonna have to agree to disagree. Then, one Sunday afternoon, we were playing the Washington Redskins, our division rivals, in a big game in Texas Stadium. We had the ball on the 45-yard line at a crucial part of the game and it was third down and 5 yards to go. We ran a sweep to Tony Dorsett who gained 4 1/2 yards and we needed just a little over a foot for a first down. But now it was fourth down at midfield. He started to send the punt team in. I ran to the sideline and told him to call a timeout because I had an idea.

I said, "Coach, we've been running a "red left rover opposite" (the rover in this case being Doug Cosbie) formation all day and the defense has started to anticipate the snap count. Every time we ran this formation, we snapped the ball with the third tight end in motion. Then when he got right behind the tackle, we always snapped it on "two" (the second "hut"). The last time we ran it, one of the defensive linemen for the Redskins anticipated the snap count and beat us across the line of scrimmage. So I said, "Let me go out and run that same formation and accentuate the second hut but we won't snap the ball and see if we can get them to jump offsides."

He thought for a few seconds and then said, "You know, that's not a bad idea but you have to promise me one thing. Under no circumstances do you snap the ball. If they don't jump offsides you just let the play clock run out. We'll take a 5-yard "delay of game" penalty and punt the football. I agreed and ran back out into the huddle. I told all the players what we were going to do. And that, "Under no circumstances are we going to snap the ball."

We broke the huddle and ran to the line of scrimmage. The Redskins were in a very unbalanced defense, and I thought, "Boy wouldn't it be nice if we had called a play off left tackle because we only need 6 inches for a first down and it would easily result in that if not a lot more. Then I realized we actually did have that play—it was a slant 36. And we had an audible system in our offense where I could change the play at the line of scrimmage using a live color. That week the live color was green so if I yelled "red 55" or "black 22" it meant nothing, just a "dummy" audible. But if I yelled "green," it meant that everything we said in the huddle was canceled and whatever followed was the new play. Out of my mouth, without even thinking about it, came "Green 36" and I repeated it about three times just so that everybody knew that we were running slant 36 and that everything I said in the huddle was canceled.

We snapped the ball and the Redskins defense beat us across the line of scrimmage, tackling our fullback in the backfield for about a 4-yard loss. There was hesitation on the part of some of our linemen, and we didn't make our blocks. I had told them in the huddle that under no circumstances would we snap the ball. Then I called a live audible so they weren't sure what we were doing. Hesitation will kill you every time in a short yardage or goal line situation. You must beat them off the snap. So, the Redskins got the ball, scored a touchdown, and ended up winning the game. I ran to the sideline in great frustration and said to Coach Landry, "Don't say anything to me until you've seen the film and I'll bet you would've done the same thing."

The newspaper the next morning had Coach Landry looking more discombobulated, mouth open and hat askew, than anyone had ever seen him. "No, Danny, no!!" was the exclamation in the captions. That day, after watching film, I was sitting in Coach Landry's office when he came in from the film room.

I said, "Okay, Coach, you've seen the film. You tell me that you wouldn't have done the same thing that I did."

He looked at me and said, "Dan, you're right. It was the perfect play to run against that defense. It should've not only gained the first down but probably should've scored a touchdown. However, I would not have done what you did. Because, you see, I understand the most important thing in a football game is not to know *why* you do something or *what* to do but rather WHEN to do it."

I realized then that he was telling me that even though that play had a 99% chance of success you don't take that 1% chance of failure when the game is on the line. At that point, I was embarrassed even further, if that was possible. As I was walking out of his office, he stopped me and said, "Hey, Dan."

Dejectedly, I turned around and said, "Yeah, Coach?"

"Don't ever change the way you play football."

His words immediately restored my confidence in myself and the way I played football. This was classic Tom Landry. He was a master teacher. He knew exactly how to turn a young quarterback's embarrassment to not only a teaching tool but a motivating one as well. It also helped tremendously to know that he knew there were a lot of times when that kind of aggressiveness and decision-making had won football games for us. Most of the time, however, that didn't make the headlines in the newspaper because they don't report planes that land safely.

HJ

Deep in the eighties, we were a relatively typical American household where kids got spanked. I would like to remember that my brothers got it more, but I've got some vivid memories I can't refute. There was *never* violence in the moment. If we were caught doing something naughty, Mom (usually) would calmly walk us away to a room and inform us we were going to "get a spanking." She would leave us then, alone in our miserable thoughts.

What seemed like an eternity later, she would enter the room with a worn wooden spoon, put us over her knee and do the deed. Afterward, we would talk it out. The apprehension was always the worst part. The best part was her hug afterward. Somehow, I left each spanking feeling more loved than before.

One day, in particular, I was awaiting my fate in her bedroom only to be surprised when Dad walked in. He'd been summoned as her replacement. His unexpected entry left me terrified, mostly because I wasn't sure if his version of discipline would be better or worse. He was so much stronger, but he was my Daddy! Could he really follow through with spanking his little girl?

No, he could not. He muttered something like, 'just don't do it again' and 'don't tell Mom I couldn't finish the job.' And I was released unscathed.

Good parents teach their children about the importance of choices, and about the correlation between those choices and consequences. I had *great* parents. We learned a lot of lessons the hard way, and Mom and Dad let us. They didn't always mitigate those negative effects, and for that I'm thankful.

When we find ourselves in the aftermath of a poor choice, we shouldn't bury our head in the sand. People in the public eye learn this quickly because they don't have the luxury. There's no sand, only cameras. They learn the best follow up is to acknowledge the blunder and ask two questions:

1. What can I learn from this? Mistakes are the most constructive teachers. If you dismiss them too quickly, you'll miss vital opportunities for growth. Every organic thing on this earth is in a process, it's either growing or decaying. Make sure you're moving in a positive direction by using every experience as a life lesson. The world only spins one direction. Hitch a ride.

2. Where do I go from here? Mistakes are singular events, one-time choices (unless you choose to repeat them.) This means they don't have to keep you in chains. They are past. Keep them there and only revisit them for inspiration to change. If a mess-up is slowing you down in the present, that's because you're letting it control you. You control you, remember?

Bred to be a perfectionist, I've had to train myself to identify the things I can control and those I can't. Once I let go of things outside my influence, I'm able to celebrate progress rather than criticizing myself when goals aren't met. As a coach as opposed to a therapist, I'm under an ethical obligation to *not* talk about the past. I actually love that limitation because it forces me to be firm with clients about looking forward and not backward. Our past is important in its influence but should not be a controlling factor.

Influences

HJ
The remainder of this book will be spotted with quotations and poems Dad has committed to memory. Our family has adopted and embraced them as mantras. These first three influenced his career in the NFL tremendously.

The Critic
Theodore Roosevelt

"It is not the critic who counts; not the man who points out how the strong man stumbles or where the doer of deeds could have done better. The credit belongs to the man who is actually in the arena, whose face is marred by dust and sweat and blood, who strives valiantly, who errs and comes up short again and again, because there is no effort without error or shortcoming, but who knows the great enthusiasms, the great devotions, who spends himself in a worthy cause; who, at the best, knows, in the end, the triumph of high achievement, and who, at the worst, if he fails, at least he fails while daring greatly, so that his place shall never be with those cold and timid souls who knew neither victory nor defeat."

DW
It's easy to get caught up in praise and hearing how great you are, but I hate exaggerated hype. It seems like everyone is selling something or has an agenda.

Every year there is an increasingly great amount of talk surrounding the draft and the combine, and the new players coming out of college. By the time the season rolls around all thirty-two teams believe they have a chance to win the Super Bowl, mostly based on talk and hype. Every team looks great on paper. But football is not played on paper.

The games begin and for thirty-one of those teams, over the next twenty weeks that belief evaporates. Injuries, mistakes, and just plain bad luck take over and the team that can avoid the curse of the football gods wins the Super Bowl.

One of the things I love about the world of sports, especially football, is that sooner or later you have to step on the field and play the game. Unlike politics and other industries, where you can literally talk your way to the top without producing anything, sports requires performance.

Unfortunately, we live in a world where exaggeration is rewarded and where sensationalism sells. It's probably why I've not been more successful as a football analyst. The best announcers aren't necessarily the best scholars of the game, they're the best orators. Say something with flair and it must be true—that's the platform of producers. Filling airtime with hot air isn't something I'm good at. Today, my only real connection to sports is as a commentator and for the reasons above, I will never be great at it. I would much rather play or coach than commentate. I would rather be "in the arena."

Hype aside, being a celebrity has its perks. There were five or six years that represent the pinnacle of my career, when I was on the top of the ladder. Like with the Christmas video mentioned earlier, I was able, because of my notoriety, to raise money for some worthy causes. Another one of those opportunities was hosting a golf tournament for the Circle Ten Council of the Boy Scouts of America. For ten years we brought a bunch of celebrities into town to not only play golf but also perform at a concert on the night of the golf tournament. It was one of the real highlights of my time in Dallas and we were able to donate a lot of money to some very worthy charities. Bill Gamble was the executive director of the Circle Ten Council and became a dear friend of mine through that experience. I also had the opportunity to record my own country music album called Country Cowboy. I was not a great singer, but this was one the highlights of my musical career. Being in the studio at Sun Records (one of Elvis Presley's stomping grounds) with some great musicians was a dream come true. One of the cuts from the album was "You're a Part of Me" that I sang with Linda Nail, an aspiring Nashville singer. That song hit number 36 on the Billboard charts. These things would not have been nearly as successful or even possible without the attention I got from being in the spotlight of fame as a result of my success on the football field.

But stepping out of the celebrity circle and away from the spotlight all these years has reinforced the sentiment that I'm not a fan of propaganda and publicity. I don't miss the headlines, good or bad. Both the criticism and the praise alike, with all their sensationalism and exaggeration are perceived by me for what they truly are — superficial, a vapor. Temporary highs and lows.

Since my retirement I've been trying my best to avoid hype and sensationalism. I don't have nearly as many "friends". I don't go to as many banquets, parties, or social gatherings. It's important to avoid things that feed your ego…to lean instead, toward real and lasting things that feed your soul.

There came a point in my career when I needed to step out of the spotlight. When Jerry Jones bought the Cowboys, as much as I would have loved to play for a team owned by him, it was time. I had climbed one ladder of life all the way to the top. I sat at a pinnacle few people get to reach. Now I've climbed down that ladder and am climbing a completely different ladder, one that will sustain me permanently. But coming down from that first ladder has been perhaps the most difficult thing I've ever done.

With Linda Nail (duets on album) at Dukes in Tulsa at my one and only live performance.

HJ

"The bubble of fame is hollow." That phrase comes from a poem Dad pulls out each Mother's Day. Unlike him, I can see so much potential benefit to having adoring fans. It's the advocate in me, I guess. But there are two types of hype. One is contrived, the other sincere. He has experienced hype that is, well, hollow.

Humans put unnecessary emphasis on *status*. We build hierarchies a little too readily. I've developed a nose for people who would be a little less involved in our lives were it not for Dad's celebrity. When it comes to first impressions, I've also developed an immediate distaste for people who give their own endorsements by over-sharing their accolades and associations. What are they up to? Confidence speaks for itself. Let it. Feigned humility is easy to spot and quickly turns my distaste to distrust. It closes a door. Dan Seals sang it best, "Everything that glitters is not gold."

My mom's father gifted her an exquisite Rolex watch. It's truly breathtaking, diamond and platinum lined with an original Rolex movement. She made an incredibly expensive mistake after only having it a few years. She took it to a jeweler who replaced the movement and returned it to her with an imitation.

At a glance, it was the same watch. But while the casing and façade of the watch were beyond impressive, the real worth was in the movement. She picked it up from the jeweler and had taken it home before recognizing the counterfeit interior. In hopes for some integrity and a settlement, she returned to the jeweler's store. He was gone. Out of business, gone. He'd hit the jackpot and was in the wind.

I still have the watch. It's a stunner. But its value is significantly reduced because of what was supplanted. Aside from the obvious analogy of 'it's what's on the inside that counts' there are deeper lessons in the Rolex.

This particular watchmaker has been dedicated to the science of horology for over a hundred years. They're in the long game. Purchasing a Rolex is actually an investment. There are only a handful of watch brands that appreciate over time and these guys are at the helm.

Plenty of factors support the status of Rolex, but here are a couple impressive facts. Many parts of the manufacturing process are done by hand, the entire process taking about a year. The movement is declared to keep accurate time for several lifetimes, no batteries included. The steel used by these guys far surpasses the luxury industry standard—not only stronger than most steels used in watches but also much less corrosive and totally water resistant.

My watch was made in a week, won't last 24 hours without needing a charge, and I certainly won't be taking it swimming.

Morals of the story:

- Finer things involve a human element.
- When you find something of significant value, play the long game.
- Frequently remind yourself where worth lies.
- If you treasure it, be careful who handles it.
- It's the movement that matters.

My brother Reed noted that our parents were two people never meant for the spotlight but placed squarely in it. I will always be grateful for the effort they spent protecting us from the public eye and the caution they instilled in us.

Casey at the Bat
Ernest Lawrence Thayer
(with epilogue by DW)
"The outlook wasn't brilliant for the Mudville nine that day;
The score stood four to two with but one inning more to play.
And then when Cooney died at first, and Barrows did the same,
A sickly silence fell upon the patrons of the game.

A straggling few got up to go in deep despair. The rest
Clung to that hope which springs eternal in the human breast;
They thought if only Casey could but get a whack at that —
We'd put up even money now with Casey at the bat.

But Flynn preceded Casey, as did also Jimmy Blake,
And the former was a lulu and the latter was a cake;
So upon that stricken multitude grim melancholy sat,
For there seemed but little chance of Casey's getting to the bat.

But Flynn let drive a single, to the wonderment of all,
And Blake, the much despised, tore the cover off the ball;
And when the dust had lifted, and men saw what had occurred,
There was Jimmy safe at second and Flynn a-hugging third.

Then from 5,000 throats and more there rose a lusty yell;
It rumbled through the valley, it rattled in the dell;
It knocked upon the mountain and recoiled upon the flat,
For Casey, mighty Casey, was advancing to the bat.

There was ease in Casey's manner as he stepped into his place;
There was pride in Casey's bearing and a smile on Casey's face.
And when, responding to the cheers, he lightly doffed his hat,
No stranger in the crowd could doubt 'twas Casey at the bat.

Ten thousand eyes were on him as he rubbed his hands with dirt;
Five thousand tongues applauded when he wiped them on his shirt.
Then while the writhing pitcher ground the ball into his hip,
Defiance gleamed in Casey's eye, a sneer curled Casey's lip.

And now the leather-covered sphere came hurtling through the air,
And Casey stood a-watching it in haughty grandeur there.
Close by the sturdy batsman the ball unheeded sped —
"That ain't my style," said Casey. "Strike one," the umpire said.

From the benches, black with people, there went up a muffled roar,
Like the beating of the storm-waves on a stern and distant shore.
"Kill him! Kill the umpire!" shouted someone on the stand;
And it's likely they'd have killed him had not Casey raised his
hand.

With a smile of Christian charity great Casey's visage shone;
He stilled the rising tumult; he bade the game go on;
He signaled to the pitcher, and once more the spheroid flew;
But Casey still ignored it, and the umpire said, "Strike two."

"Fraud!" cried the maddened thousands, and echo answered
fraud;
But one scornful look from Casey and the audience was awed.
They saw his face grow stern and cold, they saw his muscles
strain,
And they knew that Casey wouldn't let that ball go by again.

The sneer is gone from Casey's lip, his teeth are clinched in hate;
He pounds with cruel violence his bat upon the plate.
And now the pitcher holds the ball, and now he lets it go,
And now the air is shattered by the force of Casey's blow.

Oh, somewhere in this favored land the sun is shining bright;
The band is playing somewhere, and somewhere hearts are light,
And somewhere men are laughing, and somewhere children shout;
But there is no joy in Mudville — mighty Casey has struck out."

DW

I have never liked the way "Casey" ends. With respect
to Ernest Thayer, I gave this story an addendum. My own
epilogue, if you will.

As the stunned crowd watched this giant man fell crumpled to the ground,
And then he stirred and then he rose and then he rushed the mound.
The startled pitcher braced in preparation for the blow,
But Casey stopped and off'd his hand in the greatest sportsman's show.

As unfamiliar tears made tracks down Casey's tarnished face,
The huge crowd stood and roared and now their cheers consumed the place.
For Casey grew more in this single moment of defeat, than he could have if he'd ripped the ball clean out into the street.

The world we know says Casey lost, and his opponent won,
But in defeat he did more good than the winner could have done.
And other men, as Casey did, have risen to the call.
They've fought the fight. They've run the race knowing they might fall.

But the score that really counts is not the one in center field,
Or the headlines in the paper, or reports the critics yield.
For Casey gave his best, and from a challenge would not run,
On the Scoreboard in the Sky, we find…Casey really won.

The sportsmanship trophy was never the most cherished one at the banquet, at least not for me. My competitiveness came from my dad. I've watched many ping-pong paddles go flying off into the darkness after I beat my dad in a close game on the back patio at night. I also watched one fly into the wall in the dorm at California Lutheran University on the opening night of training camp my rookie year. Roger Staubach was the king of the ping-pong table at training camp, which I hadn't known previously. I learned that night for the first time (certainly not the last) that Roger does not like to lose. So you see, my father and my mentor were the two most competitive men I've ever met in my life. Between my DNA and my environment, I had no chance at being anything other than hyper competitive.

Losing with grace and class is one of the hardest things I've had to learn to do. But I'd be dishonest if I didn't admit I learned more from failing and losing than I ever did from winning. As I look back on my life, I remember the failures, the disappointments, the losses like they happened yesterday.

I think one of my greatest gifts is the ability to learn from the failures of others without having to go through them myself. I would watch Roger like a hawk. When he made a mistake (believe it or not, he did make a few) I saw it and learned from it. His greatness in my opinion, was the fact that he could make a mistake and somehow turn it into a success. He could throw a ball into triple coverage, and somehow it would be completed. The "Hail Mary" was such a play. Not a great throw, but somehow it became one of the most iconic plays in the history of the NFL.

Roger was a terrific quarterback and made a lot of great throws, but his ability to *will* a play or a game in his favor was his greatest asset.

So yes, I've always been very competitive. Too competitive. For me, the best way to get over a bad loss, and they were all bad, was to realize that my wife was waiting for me at home. It would always hit me some time on the drive or plane ride home. She loved me just as much whether we won or lost. As the kids came along, they just added to it. It made me ashamed that I let something as insignificant as a football game make me that angry.

I think the thing that hurt the most was to know that the kids had to go to school the next day and face all the teasing from the other kids that their dad lost the game for the Cowboys. The problem was, they were right. I did lose the game. Every game we ever lost, as the quarterback, I was the reason. If I had played better, we would've won. Except for one. The Chicago Bears beat us 44-0 in 1985 in Texas Stadium and I got knocked out of the game twice. I am not taking the blame for that one.

HJ

I lived in a cocoon, I think. In the days before cell phones and social media it was easier to avoid all the slander and praise that comes with fame, and I've always enjoyed the protection privacy offers anyway. I'm thankful for that time period and can only imagine the level of repute celebrities endure in today's spotlight. I was oblivious to the newspapers and radio shows and Dad was great about not bringing work home.

That said, the Dallas Cowboys team of the '80s was an icon. Branded "America's Team," public scrutiny of its many members was inevitable, and we were right there in the middle of it. Husband and wife with four small children, just trying to live like normal people.

Our parents did an exceptional job making our home life feel normal. We had plenty of chores, bus rides to school, playdates with friends, and, of course, the daily forced piano practices. But there were hints of that metaphorical microscope hovering over us — prank calls after bad games, extra attention from schoolteachers, and the occasional trespasser with cameras.

Going out in public with Dad was virtually impossible. He would try the incognito sunglasses/ball-cap combo but was still recognizable. And once one person noticed him, it was useless trying to hide.

Dad seemed impervious to it. He was resilient and able to brush things off so easily, it seemed. There was plenty of praise to balance the scale. I realize now how much worse that glaring public eye could have been for us, though. I often wonder how much slander and scrutiny I was oblivious to. I have created an image in my mind of our parents, our mother in particular, standing in front of us, holding a proverbial shield and taking the brunt. I'm sure I only know a fraction of the critiquing they both endured.

"Brilliant spirits will always encounter violent objections from mediocre minds."

Albert Einstein

DW

The game itself was the reward for all the work, effort, and pain...when we won. As mentioned, I really hated to lose. When I joined the Dallas Cowboys, one of the things that shocked me the most was how horrible it felt in the locker room the week after a loss. The pain, anger, and disappointment was almost palpable. Not to mention the plane ride home from a road game after a loss. But the worst part about losing was the critics. Losses brought them out of the woodwork.

I would answer to Coach Landry, any time or place, but to stand up at a podium after a loss and be questioned (when I was already in a bad mood) by a reporter who had never played a down of football, was difficult to bear. It was the toughest part of my career as a professional football player. When the league instituted a policy allowing media into the locker rooms after games, I complained to Coach Landry. His response was, "Never get on the wrong side of people who buy ink by the barrel."

In 1994, I was the head coach of the Arizona Rattlers in the Arena Football League. According to the media, we didn't stand a chance against the Orlando Predators in the Arena Bowl in Orlando. In fact, we were 15-point underdogs. However, we had a group of players who didn't care what the reporters thought. They simply went out and played the game and beat the Predators 36-31. I'll never forget the feeling that came over me as I watched that last pass get knocked to the ground by one of our defensive backs. We had pulled off a miraculous upset. It was maybe the greatest feeling I've ever had in football. Even though I didn't play in the game, as the head coach I felt a responsibility I couldn't have ever felt as an individual player. Watching a group of men go out and execute a game plan that I had created, was unlike any feeling I ever had as a player, made sweeter by the fact that nobody thought we stood a chance.

HJ

Einstein's summation is among Dad's favorite quotes, and one he referenced readily. It came in handy when I was in high school and got dragged into the America's Junior Miss Program. I'm definitely not the beauty queen type, didn't even know how to walk in heels, but the potential for scholarship money really beckoned. Besides, my friends were doing it.

Near the end of the program, there was an on-stage interview. The judges selected an undisclosed question for each candidate, and she had to answer on the spot, in front of the crowd. I was prepared for a question like, "What's the perfect date" when I got, "Which historical figure do you identify with and why?" I don't know how long I gaped. The pause felt substantial. Then Albert came in clutch. I recited the quote effortlessly and mumbled something about how Einstein-esque I was. Admittedly, I missed the interpretation and flubbed the comparison, but the judges didn't seem to care. They gave me a medal.

This quote speaks for itself. If someone is on the right track of a big idea, there will be opposition. Holding on to this understanding when objections hit can add fuel rather than brakes to your momentum.

When truly driven, Dad and I both figure it's a sure sign we are onto something great when stumbling blocks appear. They indicate we have something worth opposing, so we've come to expect and then embrace them.

FRIENDS

Key to Success

DW

I had a chance to sit down with Coach Landry one time and asked him what he felt the key to his football success was. He pulled out a piece of paper, drew a circle on it, and put about a dozen dots evenly spaced in the circle. Then he wrote "SB" on the outside of the circle at about twelve o'clock. He then drew a line from the middle of the circle to the 3:00 spot and then around to the "SB". Next, he said, "The circle is the team, the SB is the goal (Super Bowl), and the dots are the players. The line from the center of the circle to the 'SB' is the path we have chosen to take to reach our goal, the "Dallas Cowboys Path." It represents our philosophy. There will be thirty-two such philosophies in the NFL, all of them a little bit different.

He then drew a line from each dot beginning with the first one to the line running from the center of the circle to the three o'clock spot. Once he got five or six dots connected to the line he stopped. He said, "Those dots represent the players that have bought into the philosophy 100%. If this circle was a molecule, scientist's have told us that it is full of charged particles (the dots). Those are the players. They also tell us that through an electron microscope you can physically move those particles. And when you get enough of them in a straight line, the rest of them will fall into line without any force being applied to them. The point at which that happens is called "critical mass."

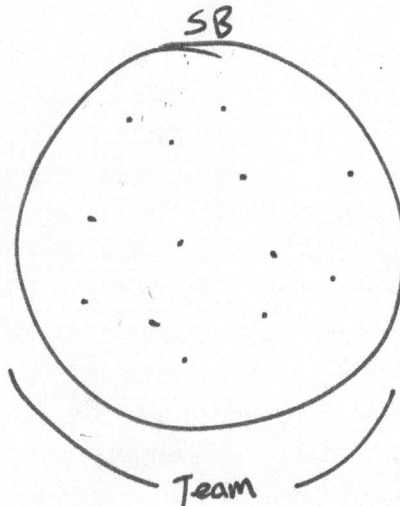

SB

Team

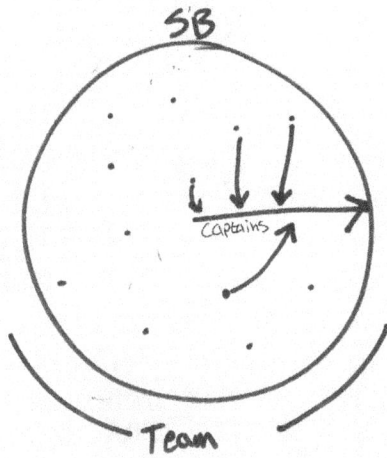

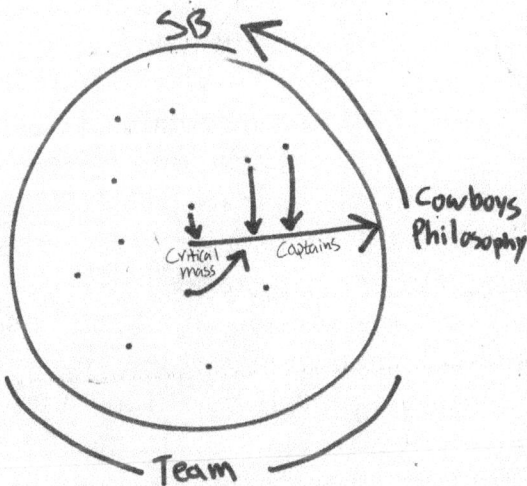

He stopped talking, and I asked, "What does this have

to do with your success?"

"Every successful team I've been a part of had great leadership amongst the players. Those first five or six dots represent the best leaders on the team. You then must empower those leaders. I do it by making them captains and letting them make important decisions regarding the team," he explained.

Things like how we dressed for road games on the plane or what we wore at practice on certain days, full pads or half pads, or just T-shirts, as well as game balls, and awards that were given to the players were all significant decisions. Being a captain was not an insignificant thing. This was how he created the environment that so many of us benefited from. An environment where ordinary football players could become Super Bowl champions. It was the collective influence and example set by the Staubach's and the Jordan's and the Renfro's and the Newhouse's and the Harris's and the Breunig's and the Pugh's.

I was confused. "But Coach, the players selected the captains, not you. We vote for the captains every year."

He said, "You're right. But who counted the votes?"

I just grinned because I knew he counted the votes. He personally hand-picked the captains. He said, "The key to my success has always been finding those key leaders that can lead us to critical mass."

Coach Landry's philosophy was always based on out-working, out-studying, and just being smarter and better conditioned than our opponent. A shared vision with adequate preparation was the key, physically and mentally. He chose players that fit that mold rather than simply looking for the biggest, strongest, fastest players he could find. He would then put together a coaching staff and an administration that worked well with those types of players. That was his key to success.

I believe that this principle has critical, potentially life-altering effects on all of us. We will only go as far as our team will take us. We will be a product of the people we surround ourselves with. So if you look around at those closest to you, it's like looking into a mirror twenty years down the road. I think this especially applies to young people.

I had great friends growing up, with the same priorities and general beliefs as I did and as my parents had taught me. Fortunately for me, my friend group started with my parents and siblings. They were the ones I was around the most, and who had the most influence on me. But I realize now that I was one of the lucky ones. Everyone is not so fortunate.

To have parents who loved me and would do anything for me, even above their own interests, was a great blessing. But I also believe that they tried not to spoil me—not to do things for me that I could do for myself. I believe (although I can't say I adhered to that belief when I was young) that when you do something for someone else, especially a child, that they can do for themselves, you have done a disservice to them. You have taken away from them an opportunity to grow, to learn, and to progress. You weaken that person. It's really hard to watch someone you love struggle. You want to do it *for* them.

Coach Landry did not micromanage the team. He chose the right leaders, empowered them, and then let them run the team. He even let them make mistakes because that's the best way to learn. By making mistakes they learned to make necessary changes, ensuring that mistakes didn't get repeated. That was part of his genius.

HJ

Tom Landry was an incredible leader. He knew how to build and leverage relationships, ensuring each member's role supported the common goal. And just like my disciplinarian parents, he wisely allowed the mess-ups to be the teachers.

Our relationships are perhaps the biggest contributing factor of who we become in life. As evidence, note how most of the lessons in this book are based on a relationship. Growing up with some walls built around me, I learned to analyze the types of relationships that are beneficial and those that aren't. If I learned anything about those associations from the sports world it's that there's a combination of varied relationships that create optimal balance in an individual's life. The following combination is our version of Coach Landry's "Key to Success."

We need coaches. We need teammates. And we need fans.

Coaches

DW

I believe the success I attained in my football career was fueled by two key factors. I gave the best I had. Always. Every practice, every game, every work-out, I did my very best. I wasn't perfect, but I was all in. Two, I was always surrounded by greatness, including my parents and family, friends, teammates, and coaches.

The most impactful experience I had with a coach, however, had nothing to do with football.

There were a few years in my life when I was really a big shot. Living in Dallas, Texas and being the quarterback for America's team, put me squarely in the spotlight. I was making a lot of money, living in a beautiful home, with a beautiful family, and had a lot of toys—a nice truck, a motorhome, a tennis court, and swimming pool.

In fact, one year I decided I wanted to have my own airplane and learn how to fly. I enrolled in a flight school, met all the requirements, and got my pilot's license. My instructor was Oscar Martinez, and he was great. He was a pilot for American Airlines and taught beginners like me in his spare time. I trained in a Cessna 150 and flew out of the McKinney Municipal Airport, north of Dallas.

A 150 is a very small, simple airplane with one engine and fixed landing gear. It wasn't very fast. In fact, on my cross country flight (the last requirement for getting your pilot's license) I was flying from McKinney to Tulsa, Oklahoma on the first leg. It just so happened that there was a pretty strong Blue Norther coming. (That's a storm front that comes from north to south and often appears blue to the eye.) I was flying directly into about a 60-knot headwind. A couple of times I looked down at the ground and the cars on the highway were actually going faster than I was.

HJ

Flying with Dad was exhilarating, especially when he would let us take the yoke! I never realized what a special opportunity it was to share a seat in a cockpit. There are countless lessons to be learned with flying, and as I look back, I cherish the insight gained from those experiences. For a kid though, it was simply an oblivious delight. My favorite trips were when we would fly to Krum, Texas for dinner at one of our favorite restaurants, The Clay Pot. (*DW*: I was totally showing off. It was only 50 miles door to door. We could have driven there faster.) They served their drinks in mason jars and had the yummiest cheese crisps.

DW

After I got my license, I was able to finally purchase a Beechcraft Baron from my father-in-law who had been a pilot all of his life. The day came when I was to take delivery of the airplane and I was like a kid on Christmas morning. It was supposed to arrive at three o'clock in the afternoon, so I called Oscar and asked him to meet me at the McKinney airport and go up with me the first time I flew it.

I was standing outside the terminal when my beautiful new toy arrived. I can't even begin to tell you how thrilled I was to watch it taxiing up to the terminal and knowing it was mine. It was red on the bottom and white on the top—with two 300 hp engines. It was absolutely gorgeous.

The delivery pilot shut it down and Oscar and I boarded it immediately. We taxied down to the end of the runway and got set up for takeoff. Once we were cleared, I pushed two throttles forward and felt like I was being shot out of a cannon. The power was unbelievable. I had never felt anything like that. Oscar must've thought I had lost my mind. We flew around North Texas for about an hour before Oscar said it was time to go back even though I didn't want to.

We got into the flight pattern on the downwind side and Oscar immediately said to me, "Have you got GUMPS?" Gumps is an acronym for a pilot's checklist, and it stands for Gas, Undercarriage, Mixture, and Props. The gas must be on the main tank (there are tanks in both of the wings as well), the undercarriage (the wheels) must be down, the mixture must be rich, and the props must be feathered properly. I went through the checklist and said to Oscar, "I have GUMPS."

We then turned on the base leg and again Oscar asked, "Have you got GUMPS?" I checked again and replied, "Got GUMPS." Finally, we turned on the final approach leg and he said once more, "Have you got GUMPS?" I felt the tank lever with my hand. It was on the main tank. I checked the landing gear lever, the mixture switch, and the props. And once again I replied with some finality, "Got GUMPS!" We were just coming up on the runway and I was slowing the airplane down as we were about to touchdown. We were about ten feet off the ground when I felt Oscar's hand on top of mine on the throttle. He then said, "I have the airplane."

Oscar had taught me if that ever happened, I was not to say anything but simply take my hand off the throttle and let him take over, which is exactly what I did. He pushed the throttle forward and we lifted back up into the air. I immediately went into panic mode. What just happened? What did I do wrong? Was something or someone on the runway? We got back in the pattern, he turned to me and said, very emphatically, "HAVE YOU GOT...GUMPS." I immediately started back through the checklist: Gas on main tank? Check. Undercarriage? Oh my gosh. It was *up*!

The Cessna I trained in had fixed gear. The wheels were not retractable and so were always down. In my training I just *pretended* to push the lever that put the wheels down. And that's exactly what I had just done, pretended. Oscar let me get ten feet away from disaster—from crash landing my beautiful red and white Beech Baron on its belly, and possibly killing us both. I immediately broke out in a cold sweat. I had Oscar land the plane because I was shaking too badly.

He told me that it was actually a good experience in a way because I would never make that mistake again. And he was right. Every time I landed my Baron after that I remembered GUMPS.

I have often thought about my experience with Oscar and my new Baron. I shudder to think what would have happened if Oscar was not with me that day. It's forced me to evaluate who my co-pilots are in everyday life? What safeguards do I have against potential disasters?

Who is going to ask me if I've got GUMPS? We need to make sure that wherever we go and whatever we do, it's somewhere and something our Coach would approve of.

HJ

Good coaches are skilled trainers who have been where you've been and have the tools to use that experience to assist you in your development. They share your enthusiasm, prepare you for what's to come, remind you of your training, allow you to learn the hard way when necessary and jump in only when you need rescuing.

Ivy was feeling extra energy one day and thought to herself, 'I think I could do a backflip on the trampoline.' She ran out, climbed up, and did a backflip. No training, no technicalities, just the stuff kids are made of. She did at least a hundred backflips before the summer was over. Then winter came. She got out of the habit.

When spring came, it was time to jump and flip again. Only this time she couldn't do it. Every time she'd start the flip, she would get scared. No amount of coaxing or coaching would budge her. Fear won.

Fear won, until her big brother Wil stepped in. First, he asked her what she was afraid of.

"Getting a concussion," she said.

"I've had concussions without even knowing I got them, Ivy. And there's nothing hard for you to hit your head on anyway." Next, he climbed up on the tramp with her and fell in sync with her jumping. He put one hand on her back and readied his other hand. "I've got you," he reassured.

They counted together, one, two, three, flip. And there it was. After a couple successful flips, he put his hands at the ready and said, "See? You've got this." On the count of three he pulled away. And you can guess what happened. She landed successfully before realizing he hadn't helped that time.

Sometimes we need a little help. We need someone to match our energy, shine light on our fears so that we can take control of them, and then actually jump in, not coach from the sidelines. We need someone who will line up next to us so they can take us from "I've got you" to "You've got this."

I've found a coach can only be successful when their subject is willing, able, and humble. If any of those qualities are missing, there won't be sustainable influence, no matter how gifted the coach.

The coach's job also hinges on the client or athlete's desire to improve. Sometimes a coach is hired by an involved third party—the parent of a wayward child— the trainer of a gifted but defiant athlete. These are often less successful clients because they didn't seek coaching on their own. In these cases, the client will only improve once they engage. No coach, no matter the skill, can influence someone without their permission.

Above all is humility. It begins with a respect for and value of what the coach has to offer. There is also undoubtedly a thickness of skin necessary when it comes to critical instruction. Coachability is neither combative nor offendable. When instruction is given, there's no argument or push-back. Imagine if Dad hadn't respected the authority of Oscar when he declared, "I have the plane." What if he'd protested, "No, no I can handle it, really." Or questioned, "Why, what's the problem?" Humility underlies all the other qualities and is a critical characteristic of a coachable student.

Danny White had all the hallmarks of a coachable athlete. He was willing, able, and humble. How many professionals can honestly say they gave 100% in their career? He left it all on the field. That, more than anything, is what helped the stars align for him.

Notes for Coaches:

- Imposing expectations on other people is a toxic trait. It's the student's job to establish their own personal expectations and your job to assist them in attaining them.
- Reward effort over achievement.
- Not everyone wants to be coached. Even when someone could use your advice, if they don't express a desire for it, there are risks in pushing forward.
- No one wants to be coached *all the time*. A level of humility is requisite for coaches as well.

The first page of Coach Landry's quarterback book stated, "The two most important words in the development of a quarterback are, *encouragement* and *praise.*" This is true of raising children, developing/ growing a company, training employees, or influencing constituents. The most successful leaders apply these two words constantly.

Teammates

HJ

In thirteen years of playing professional football, Dad only ever played for one team. That kind of relationship runs deep. Although it's been over thirty-five years since his retirement, I can't imagine cheering for anyone other than Dallas. We bleed blue. But, for Dad, what solidified his deep sense of loyalty to the Cowboys were his teammates.

DW

My teammates were men I would go to war with any time and any place, not just on the football field. I think the same is true in any group endeavor. In my life the most enjoyable accomplishments were those that I shared with others, whether in sports or business or family pursuits.

This was never truer than at an event called the "Super Teams". It was a competitive event between the two Super Bowl teams from the previous year. We met in Hawaii and competed in several non-football events, such as relay races, obstacle courses, and one that was maybe the greatest example of working together as a team that I've ever been involved in. A canoe race.

Five "rowers" sat in the canoe in a single file line. The "captain" was at the back of the boat operating the rudder. The race started at the beach and went out to and around a buoy, and then back to the beach. I was nominated to be the captain.

It was critical for the rowers to work in complete and

exact unison with each other. This would be a very close race, and any slippage of an oar or momentary lack of concentration would be the difference. If both teams stayed in sync and got the maximum speed out of their boat, the only variable would be the speed of the turn at the top of the race. That was up to me. If the turn was too sharp, the tip of the bow could cut in front of the buoy; meaning we would have to back up and go around again. That would cost us the race. If we went too wide around the turn and took too much time that could also cost us the race. I felt a tremendous amount of pressure because I was doing something I wasn't used to doing. But quarterbacks are used to pressure right? That's why I was chosen as the captain.

I played in two Super Bowls. We beat Denver in Super Bowl XII and we lost to Pittsburg in Super Bowl XIII. I was the back-up quarterback in the actual Super Bowl games and only played a couple of series when Roger broke his finger, so this canoe race was *my* Super Bowl. I was the quarterback of this Super Team. Unlike the actual football game, we won this race. And even though it's not a game that anybody will remember, to me it was huge. And to my teammates, I think it showed them I was capable of handling the pressure. At least in a canoe. Next, I had to prove it on the football field.

The point to this story, like Coach Landry's drawing of the molecule, is that football teams have to work together. I have always believed that you could take the fifty best athletes in the league and play a game against the best team in the league and the team will win every time. Synergy and chemistry on the field, in the locker room, in the community, and yes, even in a canoe, wins championships. This is also true in the home, in a business, or in just about any social or political organization. Teamwork wins.

After my retirement from the NFL, I coached in the Arena Football League for fifteen years, twelve for the Arizona Rattlers and three for the Utah Blaze, playing in five championship games and winning two of them. I learned very quickly how important it was to have good players. No matter how good you are as a coach, you can't coach a bunch of bad players into a good team. Our quarterback for most of those years was Sherdrick (Sed) Bonner, who was the best QB I ever knew who didn't play in the NFL.

In my opinion, the greatest arena football player of all time was Hunkie Cooper, and I had the privilege of coaching him. Hunkie was a coach's dream. Whenever I needed a player to take charge (because a player responds to a teammate differently than he does to a coach) Hunkie was that guy for me. He could take over a practice or a game just by sheer willpower. I'll be forever grateful that I had him on my team as a player first, and then as an assistant coach.

HJ

Quality teammates may be the most difficult to identify. We love our friends. We want them all to be good teammates but the ugly truth of it is…they may not be. Mom used to always remind me that if you go through life and only find one true friend, you're lucky! While I hope the prospects aren't quite that grim, I support the sentiment that it's wise to be careful who we surround ourselves with.

I found an ultimate example of teamwork from keeping bees. Bees are fascinating in many aspects, but one of my favorites is their model of a perfect community. No single bee can survive on its own. They survive only as a colony, each with a unique role, executed singly and efficiently, without alteration. Some of the roles include cleaning, guarding, nursing, collecting, storing, creating, caring and maintaining. Each role serves the hive, not the individual.

A team with all its members shares one common vision. When in perfect synergy, the whole actually becomes more than the sum of its parts. A true teammate knows how to lose himself in sight of the common goal and is willing to make personal sacrifices. He wants his comrades to be their best and will push them to it.

DW

In the book, "The Gates of Fire," the author, Steven Pressfield, chronicles, the life of Dienekes, one of the 300 Spartans warriors who, in 480 BC, were chosen to meet the two million Persian troops crossing the ocean to attack Western Europe.

The warriors were to meet the Persians at the Gates of Thermopylae, where the mountains formed a barrier that limited the Persians ability to come on shore. The

Spartans knew they would die in the attempt, but they also knew that the time they were fighting for was precious, allowing the Greeks to put together their forces, which eventually defeated the Persians. They fought for seven days! The king of the Persians, Xerxes, was so inspired by the efforts and ferociousness of the Spartans that, once the battle was over, instructed his captains that if they found a Spartan warrior alive that they should bring the warrior to him. On the battlefield, under an overturned cart, they found Dienekes, still breathing. They took him to the king. The king had one simple question that he was dying to ask. "What was it that made you fight so hard?" Dienekes replied,

"Nothing fires the warrior's heart more with courage than to find himself and his comrades at the point of annihilation, at the brink of being routed and overrun, and then to dredge not merely from one's own bowels or guts but from one's discipline and training the presence of mind not to panic, not to yield to the possession of despair, but instead to complete those homely acts of order which Dienekes had ever declared the supreme accomplishment of the warrior: to perform the commonplace under far-from-commonplace conditions. Not only to achieve this for oneself alone, as Achilles or the solo champions of yore, but to do it as part of a unit, to feel about oneself one's brothers-in-arms, in an instance like this of chaos and disorder, with Comrades whom one doesn't even know, with whom one has never trained — to feel them filling the spaces alongside him, from spear side and shield side, fore and rear, to behold one's comrades likewise rallying, not in a frenzy of mad possession-driven abandon, but with order and self-composure, each man knowing his role and rising to it, drawing strength from him as he draws it from them. The warrior in these moments finds himself lifted as if by the hand of a god. He cannot tell where his being leaves off and that of the comrade beside him begins. In that moment the phalanx forms a unity so dense and all-

divining that it performs not merely at the level of a machine or engine of war but, surpassing that, to the state of a single organism, a beast of one blood and heart." Dienekes; Spartan Warrior
   Steven Pressfield (Gates of Fire)

Another one of my favorite quotes. As a coach, I often had it up on the wall in locker rooms. I have used it in many keynote speeches when I wanted to show an example of what a great team consists of. This story, the story of the 300 Spartans, similar to the story of the Alamo, is one of the greatest examples I can think of when it comes to building the ultimate team. It illustrates players/warriors willing to give up their lives for a common cause.

This principle is powerful and is relevant any time you are trying to build a team — whether it be a business, a family, or any other organization where synergy is the goal, where creating an environment so a person can exceed his own potential is desired. Is that even possible? To exceed your own potential? I say it is, because it happened to me.

Because of this type of team environment, created by Coach Landry, a small baseball player from a small town was able to do things just about every young man in the world only dreams of. It was a result of being surrounded by great players and coaches who had a relentless desire to win. And we did. But none of us individually could have achieved such success. We made each other better than we ever could have been on our own.

Roger always claimed that he would not have been as good a quarterback if it hadn't been for me pushing him. I will always be grateful to him for his powerful example, and not just in being a quarterback, but in being a professional and a leader and always keeping football in its proper place.

He, Coach Landry, and several of my other teammates only confirmed what I'd been taught my entire life by my father and mother. Don't ever let football interfere with more important things in your life.

HJ

Teammates know how to build off your efforts. You'll recognize them by their focus. It'll never be on themselves.

Here are some hallmarks of the right kind of teammates:

They want you to have what you need even if it's hard on them. They want what's most important for you. That doesn't mean they always want you to have what *you* want.

They know how to build off your efforts. They compensate for your weaknesses, not by exploiting them but by leveraging them, in turn giving you their best efforts so that you can build from them with your strengths.

They challenge you in the best ways, contributing personally to your efforts, and amplifying your strengths. Like a coach, they're not afraid to hurt your feelings when it's what you need…so toughen up.

They don't look out for number one. The team is their number one. When you find someone who cares more about what's best for the team than what they want, you've found a teammate.

True teams see successes as *ours* and failures as *ours*. There's no blame nor shame, only unity. No jealousy nor comparison. The best teams and teammates accelerate the progress of their individuals and make each other better.

DW

As mentioned, one key to a quarterback's success is being surrounded by great players; an offensive line that protects him, receivers who get separation from their defenders, running backs who fight for extra yards, defenses that limit the opponents' scoring so we don't have to score as much. Every QB is measured by wins and losses and his teammates make that difference for him. Some extraordinary quarterbacks never get that opportunity simply because they're not in the right place at the right time like I was.

Both Frank Kush and Tom Landry built teams and created environments where ordinary athletes, like myself, could achieve extraordinary results. How does a skinny baseball player from Mesa, AZ end up having a thirteen-year career in the NFL and play in two Super Bowls? It simply doesn't happen for a quarterback without great teammates and coaches, because a quarterback doesn't get to do his job until others do theirs.

When I joined the Dallas Cowboys, I quickly formed a strong relationship with Roger Staubach. We had very similar ideas about football and training but also about family and priorities. I have always said that there is no position in all of sports that is more dependent on those around him than a quarterback. He can't do his job until his teammates do theirs. Contrary to public opinion, you don't start building a team with a quarterback. You end with the quarterback.

Every day we competed in something—basketball, tennis, sprinting, and working out in general. We were closely matched in terms of speed and strength. One of our competitive activities was the bench press. The Dallas Cowboys quarterback record was 300 pounds at the time and both of us had bench pressed 295 pounds but had not been able to lift 305.

One day, for some reason, I was feeling a little extra energy, so I challenged him to a competition. It happened to be the day we were maxing out. I got 295 and rather than going for 300 I decided to put 305 on and go for the record. Mustering everything I had, I actually lifted 305 pounds after which there was a roar, high fiving and congratulations between several players and me. I was especially pumped because our conditioning coach,

Bob Ward, was there. Everyone was applauding me... except Roger. He just stood there with a blank look on his face. Finally, he just turned around and stormed into the locker room. "What's wrong with Roger?" everyone was asking.

Naturally, we all thought he was angry, but it was more than that. He returned carrying a red paper Coke cup and a very determined and indignant look on his face. Nobody said a word. He tore out the bottom of the cup and slipped it onto the end of the barbell with the 305 pounds on it. He laid down on the bench and with all the strength and energy he had in his whole body he lowered the weight down to his chest and pushed it up. Red faced, head shaking and exerting every ounce of muscle, he got it! Everyone watching erupted in cheers and laughter.

I had just broken the all-time Dallas Cowboys quarterback bench press record at 305 pounds. But I only held it for a few minutes before Roger lifted 305 pounds... and a paper cup.

HJ

Dad and I attended a day camp for fathers and daughters when I was a young teen. The weather was nice, there were snacks and games, it could have been such a lovely time. But someone introduced a competition.

It was a water-balloon toss. Catching isn't my best skill. After several rounds, Dad was getting pretty frustrated with my incompetence. He was just playing around but this guy has a bit of an arm on him. He wound up and drilled me in the stomach with our last water-balloon. Unfortunately, the balloons used that day weren't the typical thin water-balloons. They were standard balloons—the heavy-duty stuff so they were hard to break. It knocked me off my feet and knocked the wind right out of me.

I wasn't happy with my teammate, and he wasn't happy with his. We weren't unified in our goal. I certainly wanted to win, but not at the expense of my ability to breathe. And winning wasn't my top priority. Did I mention there were snacks?

He wanted to win. It was a competition after all, and we should've owned it. The thing about teammates is, it's not the person that matters so much as the alignment. Do they share the same goals and focus? Thankfully, Dad and I have had other opportunities to work as a team. I think we've improved.

Fans

DW

I mentioned my dad being my biggest fan. He really was. The first time he was ever going to miss one of my games in any sport was while I was playing at ASU and we had a road game at BYU. He apologized to me the day before the game, saying he had too much work to do and wouldn't make it to Provo. It really wasn't a big deal to me, but I could tell it was killing him.

The morning of the game, I woke up early in the hotel in Provo and went down to the hotel lobby to find something to eat. What I found, instead, was my dad asleep on the couch there. I shook him awake and asked him what happened to all his work.

"Oh, I got it all done," he said. "Will you go call your mom and tell her where I am?"

Mom knew exactly where he was. He had driven nine hours (probably made it in closer to seven and a half) overnight to get there. He really couldn't ever stand to miss one of my games.

HJ

My parents are my biggest ride-or-die as well. I was playing in a basketball game one time when I stole the ball and headed for a fast break. As my defender turned, I caught her foot on mine and took a good dive, cracking my head loud on the hardwood and knocking the wind out of me...again.

The referees didn't stop the game — didn't even blow a whistle. Instead of attending to me, they were focused on the game. So, in the middle of the game, my dad stormed the court. Words were exchanged and he was asked to exit the gym.

Your biggest fans should be concerned about one thing — you.

I guess I should've said there was an *attempt* to throw him out. They weren't successful. He wasn't about to go down without a fight. He told the officials they would have to bring in the Arizona National Guard to escort him out of that gym if they really wanted him out of there.

They let him stay. I was fine by the way. Our trainer took care of me while Dad and the ref were facing off. A minor concussion and an embarrassing parent story to add to my file.

The Race
Dee Groberg

"Quit! Give Up! You're beaten!"
They shout at me and plead.
"There's just too much against you now.
This time you can't succeed."

And as I start to hang my head
In front of failure's face,
My downward fall is broken by
The memory of a race.

And hope refills my weakened will
As I recall that scene;
For just the thought of that short race
Rejuvenates my being.

A children's race—young boys, young men—
How I remember well.
Excitement, sure! But also fear;
It wasn't hard to tell.

They all lined up so full of hope
Each thought to win that race.
Or tie for first, or if not that,
At least take second place.

And fathers watched from off the side,
Each cheering for his son.
And each boy hoped to show his dad
That he would be the one.

The whistle blew and off they went
Young hearts and hopes afire.
To win and be the hero there
Was each young boy's desire.

And one boy in particular
Whose dad was in the crowd
Was running near the lead and thought:
"My dad will be so proud!"

But as they speeded down the field
Across a shallow dip,
The little boy who thought to win
Lost his step and slipped.

Trying hard to catch himself
His hands flew out to brace,
And mid the laughter of the crowd
He fell flat on his face.

So down he fell and with him hope
–He couldn't win it now–
Embarrassed, sad, he only wished
To disappear somehow.

But as he fell his dad stood up
And showed his anxious face,
Which to the boy so clearly said,
"Get up and win the race."

He quickly rose, no damage done,
–Behind a bit, that's all–
And ran with all his mind and might
To make up for his fall.

So anxious to restore himself
–To catch up and to win–
His mind went faster than his legs:
He slipped and fell again!

He wished then he had quit before
With only one disgrace.
"I'm hopeless as a runner now;
I shouldn't try to race."

But in the laughing crowd he searched
And found his father's face;
That steady look which said again:
"Get up and win the race!"

So up he jumped to try again
–Ten yards behind the last–
"If I'm to gain those yards," he thought,
"I've got to move real fast."

Exerting everything he had,
He regained eight or ten,
But trying so hard to catch the lead
He slipped and fell again!

Defeat! He lied there silently
–A tear dropped from his eye–
"There's no sense running anymore;
Three strikes: I'm out! Why try!"

The will to rise had disappeared;
All hope had fled away;
So far behind, so error prone;
A loser all the way.

"I've lost, so what's the use," he thought
"I'll live with my disgrace."
But then he thought about his dad
Who soon he'd have to face.

"Get up," an echo sounded low.
"Get up and take your place;
You were not meant for failure here.
Get up and win the race."

"With borrowed will get up," it said,
"You haven't lost at all.
For winning is no more than this:
To rise each time you fall."

So up he rose to run once more,
And with a new commit
He resolved that win or lose
At least he wouldn't quit.

Three times he'd fallen, stumbling
Three times he rose again
Still he gave it all he had
And ran as though to win.

They cheered the winning runner
As he crossed the line first place.
Head high, and proud, and happy;
No failing, no falling, no disgrace.

But when the fallen youngster
Crossed the line last place,
The crowd gave him the greater cheer,
For finishing the race.

And even though he came in last
With head bowed low, unproud,
You would have thought he'd won the race
To listen to the crowd.

And to his dad he sadly said,
"I didn't do too well."
"To me, you won," his father said.
"You rose each time you fell."

And now when things seem dark and hard
And difficult to face,
The memory of that little boy
Helps me in my race.

For all of life is like that race,
With ups and downs and all.
And all you have to do to win,
Is rise each time you fall.

"Quit! Give up! You're beaten!"
They still shout in my face.
But another voice within me says:
"GET UP AND WIN THE RACE!"

HJ
The Race has always been a favorite poem for us. We can each recite it on command. And we relate to it because we also have our own personal race story.

Ryan, my oldest brother, had heart complications all his life. The rest of us were athletes, competitors, and winners by all standards. He was the kid last picked. He struggled to even join the game.

I remember attending a track meet he was in, watching him run the half-mile with his peers. It was difficult to not be embarrassed for him. It hurt my heart to see him running because he was always and expectedly dead last. Because it was two times around the track, there was

145

a point where he had even gotten lapped by the other runners. He crossed the finish line after the victor and had to keep running because he still had a lap to go.

After the winner was declared it seemed like an eternity before Ryan crossed the finish line. Some in the crowd were annoyed they had to wait for the next event because there was this poor kid who wasn't getting off the track. I'll never forget the evident pride in his eyes when he came over to Dad, who was standing right outside the gate with a stopwatch. Ryan had been running against himself, setting his own personal time, like there was no one else even on the track.

Ryan's resilience taught us more about victory than any professional games could. Success isn't about placement, it's about movement. He isn't with us anymore, and I often wish I could have gleaned more from his perspective. I think he had the same relationship with failure as Dad. Failure was simply not trying. Anything attempted was a gain. If I had to guess his philosophy on winning it would be something like, "I'm a winner because I refuse to quit."

DW

Having had my share of failures and mishaps, the poem about the race resonates with me in more ways than one. The influence of the father being one. Like the boy in the race, I have always been driven by an extreme desire to make my dad proud of me. He had a knack for bringing me up when I was down and bringing me down when I was up. (That's a person you want by your side in life.) He knew after every game exactly what I needed. Whenever I had a really good game, he found something I could have done better, and whenever I had a bad game, he built me up.

Ryan needed me to be that person for him in his race. He was born with an atrial septal defect (a hole in the upper collecting chambers of his heart) and a leak in the mitral valve. He had surgery when he was four years old to patch the hole, but they could not fully repair the leak. As a result, he simply did not develop physically in a normal way and was not very coordinated. However, he was blessed, or cursed, with the competitiveness inherent in the White family. As a result, Ryan could not really compete in sports. In the seventh grade he wanted to be on the track team and the only event that the coaches could find that he could participate in was the half mile run or 800 meters. So at every track meet, when they lined up for the race there he was all fired up, ready to run. By the time he finished his first lap, he'd already been lapped by the other runners.

As the disappointment of losing the race set in, I tried to teach him not to compare himself to the other boys in the race, but only to compete with himself. To run each race in an attempt to beat his best time. And if he could do that, he had won. I remember one particular day at one of the first meets. I was late getting to the track and barely had time to run up to the fence surrounding it. I stood just outside of the first turn around the track. Most of the boys had finished the race but Ryan was just finishing his first lap. He looked up and saw me. His expression was full of discouragement, as if he was saying, 'What do I do?' I knew at that moment he needed a fan. I shouted over the fence my confidence in him, that I knew he could finish. Then I screamed at him, "Just one foot in front of the other!" And that became his motivation. He ran in every meet, and he never quit a race. And he usually got a standing ovation when he finished.

HJ

Why do we need fans anyway? Should we really let others' opinions of us be an influence? I say yes. Self-esteem isn't reliable and self-confidence tends to wane. Both are subject to comparison, which is never healthy. Having someone who loves you for no reason gives you wings. Not having to worry about your value being contingent on your performance — that's freeing.

Fans never say, "I told you so" when you fail. They'll say something like, "You'll get 'em next time" or "You're the coolest" and play up your strengths. They do this because they do truly, authentically, think you're the coolest.

We come by some fans naturally, like our families. Some we pick up later. Their unconditional love sustains us when life gets dicey. When frightening situations arise — and they will — we need to know who is cheering us on, even (and especially) if we're doing something risky, or plain stupid.

True, we need checks and balances, people to warn us when we're about to jump off a cliff. That's what coaches and teammates are for. But ask yourself, who's going to applaud the jump. Because we need those people too.

One last thing about *The Race.* It illustrates something important about fans. They love a comeback kid. Fans will appreciate a good recovery over a flawless execution almost every time. Win or lose, a true fan is with you completely. But show them a recovery and you'll solidify their hearts forever. And they, in turn, will be the ones hoisting you in the air when the victories do come.

Some differences should be noted.

Fans are in the stands. They're not right with you and rarely know all the intricacies of the situation. They're just there for you, rain or shine, win or lose. Cheering you on.

Teammates are in the trenches. They know your situation intimately, though they may have a little different investment or challenge. The bonds you make with them will be real and lasting.

Coaches watch closely but they're a step away. They know exactly where you've been and hold tremendous value with that perspective. Respect it and take their advice above all else. They know what it takes.

My dad has occupied each one of these roles at different times in my life, and I've done the same for him. When you find someone who can be a coach, teammate, or fan, depending on what you need at the time, there's a gem. Value them. If you can learn to distinguish these relationships in your life and how that influence matters, you'll then be able to become the right person for those who have let you occupy a sacred space in their lives.

Parable of the Kayak

DW

It's probably pretty easy to see how much value I place on the importance of being surrounded by the right people in our lives. The most important person in my life has been Jo Lynn. She and Ryan passed away within six months of each other. Needless to say, it was a very, very emotional time for me, and it changed me dramatically. Much like losing the quarterback of a football team, that influence and impact cannot be simply replaced by another person. It takes an entire team stepping up to even begin to fill the void. Such was the case with me when she left this existence and joined our loved ones in the next.

I have spent a great deal of time reading and studying and praying to gain an understanding as to where she is and what she is doing. It's a topic that I will not go into here except just to say that I have gained an unshakable testimony that she is together with those she loves, and that she is happier than she has ever been.

In 2007 we took a family trip to Hawaii to celebrate her parents' 70th wedding anniversary. One of the activities there was a kayak trip. I'm going to include her description of that event. I hope from reading it, you'll get a good idea as to the character and quality of the woman I chose as my eternal companion. It was the single greatest decision I made in my life.

This is called "The Parable of the Kayak" by Jo Lynn White.

Our adventure took place on the beautiful island of Kaua'i. Danny and I were there with family in celebration of my parents' 70th wedding anniversary. On this particular day we joined my siblings and their spouses to kayak up a river. Though I couldn't vouch for my husband's enthusiasm, I thought it was going to be great fun.

After choosing our kayak, we quietly listened as our guide gave us all the instructions. There would be two people per kayak. The woman, sitting in the front, was to set the pace by dipping her oar in the water, alternately on one side, and then the other. The man was to sit behind her. It would be his job to steer. Although his oar might occasionally stay on the same side to maneuver the kayak, he was to watch her oars, and keep in the same rhythm. The guide stressed, more than once, that our oars should be in perfect harmony with each other. Otherwise, they would collide. In kayaking terms, this is known as a "high five". We were also cautioned to stay away from the middle of the river, because often there were motorboats that would come by and be a danger to us.

The directions seemed simple enough so off we went. I remember thinking how wonderful this was going to be. The scenery was absolutely gorgeous, and we were doing something together that was different and fun. It was such a romantic setting with the sparkling water and the warm, gentle breeze blowing on our faces. We began the journey with smooth sailing, while laughing and snapping pictures of one another.

After a short while, I noticed that our kayak began to turn toward the bank of the river. I was sure Danny would straighten it out, but we kept turning until we were sideways. I didn't want to complain, and the kayak was so small that I couldn't turn around to see what happened to him, but he was obviously not doing his job.

I glanced up to see my sister, two of my brothers and their spouses. I was amazed at the ease with which they seemed to be moving in the water. The oars of each couple were in perfect sync, and they were nowhere near the banks of the river. Our oars were getting out of accord. There were times I would bring mine out of the water, and it would hit his. I thought to myself, He is very athletic, and I am fairly coordinated. What is wrong with us?

Since he wasn't doing his job the right way, I decided to fix the problem myself. Contrary to the instructions, I began to dip my oar repeatedly on the same side to steer the kayak back the other way. Our oars clinked as we gave each other some more "high-fives". But my steering over corrected the kayak and we began heading toward the middle of the river. Danny's voice got louder as he grumbled at me that he was trying to follow but couldn't tell which side I was going to paddle. We were all over the place, and at one point we even rammed into another couple's kayak. Our conversation with each other took on a new tone. However, we kept trying to get our oars back in sync. Eventually, we made enough progress to make it to the halfway point where we stopped and pulled our kayak out of the water.

It felt good to be able to get out and stretch our legs and rest for a minute. We went on a half mile hike that ended at a beautiful waterfall and swimming pool. There, we had lunch and visited. As we ate, I asked Danny why he tried to steer us to the bank of the river soon after we started. He said that if we were closer to the side, there would be less current to slow us down. It made me wonder how many times in our lives I have become annoyed with him only to find out later that his intent or idea had been good.

As it came time to head back, I thought it would be much easier. The ride would be downstream, and we had worked out the rhythm of our oars. But we hadn't been back in the kayak for five minutes when Danny started complaining that he was getting cramps in his legs. He said the kayak was too small. He needed to stretch out his legs, and his sitting position was very uncomfortable. Then the gentle breeze we had felt on the way up, had turned into an afternoon headwind. It blew so strongly against us, that if we both stopped rowing at the same time, we drifted back upstream.

Oh, how my arms began to ache! Rowing against this wind took a lot of work. It was a challenge we had not anticipated. With his cramping legs and my burning arms, it didn't seem to matter anymore whether or not we were the first to get back. As hard as this was, we didn't want to bail out. But I couldn't see how we were going to make it to the end. It was a long, hard, four-mile ride. (Although our ride was probably four and a half.)

Danny and I talk often about our excursion on the river. It has become very meaningful to us because we found many analogies to our marriage. In fact, the following Christmas he purchased a kayak oar and had our names engraved on each paddle to help remind us of what we learned from this experience.

As our kayak started, heading to the bank of the river, I can see now that it would have been better for us had I kept rowing and concentrated on the instructions given to me as part of the rowing team, instead of trying to do Danny's job. Certain roles are suited for certain people. Selfishly, trying to do things our own way leads to clanking oars and frustration.

Looking ahead and seeing the other couples rowing happily, and smoothly along, disheartened me. I know firsthand it is easy to become discouraged about our own marital relationships when we weigh it against others. Comparisons never lead to happiness.

There are many "winds" that can test a marriage. When I think about the promises Danny and I made at the altar, I feel strength and a greater desire to become one with him. Rowing against the wind, my arm muscles burned so much that often I just had to stop. But we kept moving in the water because he didn't stop. When that happened, I thought to myself, My man is so strong, and so willing to sacrifice his cramped legs and discomfort to get us back. *I couldn't let him do it alone, so I picked up my oar and started rowing again. I am sorry that I didn't tell him at the time what I was thinking. He silently motivated me to try harder.*

To initiate the building of a better relationship, I realize now that it really only takes one who is willing to work at forgiveness, to look for the good in another, to find things for which to express appreciation, and make the effort to express love. The pure love of Christ belongs in marriage more than anywhere else. The trials we face can serve to bring us closer to Jesus Christ. As we move closer to becoming like Him, we move closer to each other. We learn better how to love as He loves.

Our kayak adventure proves we are far from being the perfect couple. We have our little issues that we are still working on after all these years, but we do have the same desire for an eternal family. Our kayak made it to the end of the river. We came in far behind the others, but we made it, in spite of all the winds blowing against us. It is my testimony that the only way for peace and happiness in this life and eternity in the next is to follow our greatest Guide in His way."

Jo Lynn

FAITH

Lost

"We couldn't comprehend light were it not for the shadows."
                                                              HJ

HJ

Dad had too many surgeries to count so he got a little too casual, in my opinion, in his aftercare. One surgery on his neck he was particularly flippant with. This being a major surgery, he was going to be prone to blood clots. He had a trip planned to San Diego and wanted to drive it. From his home in Arizona, it was about six hours one way. Fortunately, he complained to his brother Chad (who had assisted as the PA in the surgery) about a pain he was having behind his left knee. His brother luckily convinced him to have it checked out before starting out for San Diego. He was admitted to the hospital upon arrival for a pulmonary embolism. The admitting doc said, whoever it was that sent you in here, thank them for saving your life. You wouldn't have made it to Yuma.

That was the first time Chad saved Dad's life.

DW

My brother Chad and I were elk hunting up on the Boquillas Ranch in Northwest Arizona, a huge cattle ranch and really rough country. With rolling hills covered with cedars, it is very rocky with cattle sparsely scattered throughout. From the looks of it you would never believe it was elk country but there are huge elk on that ranch.

One afternoon, we went out for the evening hunt but

were late leaving. We wanted to be out and set up by four o'clock, but it was right about four and we hadn't left yet so we were rushing to get out. We grabbed our gear from camp quickly, jumped in the truck, and drove to the spot we picked out, then set out in a couple of different directions.

I went out on a point and saw what I thought was a pretty good bull elk, but I couldn't get a good look at it before it went into the trees, so I started walking after it. This was territory I'd never been in before, so I was already unfamiliar with it. And with no natural landmarks and a cloudy rainy night, I was without any reference points at all.

I started following the elk tracks through the cedars, but it got dark on me fast and I lost the trail. Because we were in such a hurry to leave camp, I had no essentials with me. I've never in my life gone hunting without a flashlight, matches, and a phone (not that it would've worked because there was no signal out there) at minimum. I had nothing. There were no stars or moonlight because of cloud cover. With each blind step I didn't know if my foot would come down on a rock or in mud. A couple times I stepped in mud that reached to my ankles. It made walking extremely difficult since I couldn't see the ground underneath me.

I knew I was guessing at the direction I should be going. After trudging along for a while, I figured I might be going the wrong direction and with every step getting farther from the truck, so I found a big cedar and got under it. With the edge of my bow I started digging, hoping to get a deep enough hole that I could lay in it and stay as warm as possible through the night. Maybe if I found some branches to lay over me, I could stay somewhat dry.

As I dug, I looked up and saw headlights off in the

distance. It was in the direction I had been walking, so that was encouraging, but because it was so dark, I couldn't tell how far away those headlights were. It could've been a mile or ten miles. But I decided, since at that point I knew where a road was (there were very few roads) I would resume walking and head that direction. I started walking again.

After another hour of walking, I heard rushing water. I came to a wash running full because of the rain. I knew we had parked by a pond so I thought I would follow that water. I was also coming off surgery for a blood clot and didn't have much energy to begin with so by this point I was completely out of energy. I decided to hang my bow up in a tree and get my pack off so I could climb to higher ground. There seemed to be a hill nearby and I thought if I got up there, I would be able to hear a horn honking or someone yelling. The noise of the rushing water was preventing me from hearing anything.

I was to the point where I could take three steps then I had to rest. It would take me fifteen minutes to walk only about 100 yards. I would yell and listen, then walk fifteen minutes and yell and listen, trying to find a spot where I could see through the trees. I had done this four or five times when I heard a voice yelling. With all my strength I yelled back.

Sure enough, it was Chad. I kind of hobbled down the hill toward his voice, then I saw his flashlight on the next hill. I walked down to the bottom and Chad came running up to me. He jumped on me, but I was too tired to jump or celebrate or anything.

I found out that he'd called family members and both the Arizona Game and Fish Department, and the Forest Service were on their way because it was such a cold night. At the time I didn't think it was as cold as it was, but being wet and cold I realize now I may not have survived. Honestly, the scariest part for me was that I couldn't see. He had been out all night looking for me.

That was the first and last time I've ever been really lost. And I will never ever make the mistake of going out when there's even a chance of losing my directions, or without my flashlight, matches, and phone. I'll never do it again.

We went back for the next two days but could not find my bow. I thought I knew about where it was, but it had been so dark I really had no way of knowing where it could be. It turned out, when Chad found me, I was only a couple hundred yards from where the truck had been parked.

The following week we went back again to try to find my bow. I was walking along that wash where the water had been running, and Chad was on the other side of the wash searching. I looked down to see a piece of flagstone, pointed at one end. Later I showed it to Chad. He said someone had to have brought it in from somewhere else and put it there. Flagstone wasn't natural in that area. That's probably why it stood out to me. We figured maybe someone had used it to sit on for a blind as it was surrounded by large rocks. It was a perfect spot for scouting. But the shape of the stone was kind of oblong, and it had a very distinct point almost like an arrow on one end of it. When I followed the point of that piece of flagstone, about fifty yards away, was my bow. The flagstone was pointing directly at the tree it was hanging from, with my bag under it.

While walking through the mud and slush after I had dug the hole and seen the headlights, I kept singing to myself "Lead Kindly Light", a favorite hymn of mine. I was never really panicked or scared at all, just a bit concerned about possibly hurting my leg because I didn't know if my foot was going to come down on rock or mud.

But after talking to Chad and finding out what all happened, I kind of lost my mind thinking about what might have gone wrong. I'm glad I didn't feel that way the whole time I was out there. At the time, I was just thinking, "Oh well, I'll find the truck or he'll find me."

That experience was probably the one and only time I've known what it was like to be truly blind. I was trapped. I couldn't just turn on a flashlight or pull a blindfold off. There was no way out of a very dark world.

Chad, I owe ya……. Again.

Lead, kindly light, amid the encircling gloom
Lead thou me on
The night is dark, and I am far from home
Lead thou me on
Keep thou my feet, I do not ask to see
The distant scene, one step enough for me

HJ
My husband had his bags packed and the truck loaded. It would be an eight-hour drive by the time he would've gotten there, so news likely would've been updated. But we couldn't just sit. Chad had called me about an hour after dark in a panic and told us what was going on. My mom wasn't reachable, and it was a horrible feeling knowing he was out there, lost, and we were so far away. Luckily before we got too far down the road, Chad called back with good news.

I'm not sure if it's born of nature or nurture, but for as long as I can remember I've leaned heavily on prayer. When trouble comes, my first instinct is to hit my knees. Some call it foolish, but even if I'm wrong in the end about God's existence, it's worth the peace it gives me here and now. There's comfort in hope.

That doesn't mean I wasn't scared though. Understanding the situation as I did, I knew things could go bad very quickly and there was nothing I could do about it. Nothing, except pray.

Don't ever think you're okay on your own. Everyone needs someone, be it a friend, Deity, or a brother looking for you in a dark, damp forest. We are not meant to be alone. Like Wilbur needed Charlotte, we will need unreciprocated and unconditional help at times. Let your loved ones search and pray for you.

Note the final two verses of Lead Kindly Light.

I was not ever thus, nor prayed that thou
Shouldst lead me on.
I loved to choose, and see my path but now
Lead thou me on.
I loved the garish day, and spite of fears
Pride ruled my will, remember not past years.

So long thy power hath blest me, sure it still
Will lead me on
O'er moor and fen, o'er crag and torrent, till
The night is gone.
And with the morn those angel faces smile
Which I have loved long since and lost a while.

Loss

"Even in our sleep, pain which cannot forget falls drop by drop upon the heart until, in our own despair, against our will, comes wisdom through the awful grace of God."
                                                            Aeschylus

DW

It was August 1, 2013. I was driving down the street in Mesa when I got a phone call from my mom. She was clearly distraught and screaming on the phone, "Your father has died."

Obviously taken by surprise I said, "What?"

She said it again, "Your father has died. He had a heart attack and he's at Chandler Regional Hospital. We're headed there now."

All I could get out was, "Okay I'll meet you there." And that was it. I thought, "Did that really just happen?" Clearly now in disbelief, I don't even remember the thirty-minute drive to the hospital. I was the first one to arrive and so I had to go identify my dad in the emergency room. I can't describe in words the feeling of seeing my father's lifeless body on a gurney in the hospital. We had no warning. He'd been vibrant and healthy all his eighty-five years. In fact, he'd just mowed the lawn that very morning. That was the first time anything truly traumatic had ever happened to me. But it was the beginning of the darkest two years of my life.

HJ

Buddy was the sweetest, cutest, craziest black Labrador Retriever puppy and he was all mine! Dad was *great* with birthdays. Buddy was only a couple months old, however, when tragedy befell him. I remember exactly where I was and how it felt when I got the news. Dad called me downstairs, and I could tell he was distraught. It took him some time to find his words—which was rare. He told me he'd been in his car and was pulling out of the driveway when he felt a bump under the tire. Nothing could be done. Buddy was gone.

What I remember most about this experience is that although I was experiencing grief from losing my precious Buddy, I was more emotional from the sorrow I felt for my dad. He took full responsibility for not only Buddy's death but in tandem, my heartbreak. Sad as I was about Buddy, I couldn't bear to see Dad feeling the weight of letting me down. I remember collecting myself quickly and feigning a toughness that didn't match my feeling. I couldn't let him see how hurt I was.

Snuffles, the hamster, was my next opportunity at caregiving. She lived a full and happy life with plenty of hamster-grade experiences—playing in her exercise ball, surviving my brothers, getting lost, getting found. She had a good run. But pet owners know too well, our fur-babies don't often outlive us. When it became apparent,

166

she was on her way to hamster heaven I couldn't bear to watch her suffer. Dad took her in his patriarchal hands and explained to me in great detail how he was going to 'ease her passing' then tenderly dispose of her remains. I felt assured of his proficiency in hamster anatomy, said my goodbyes and walked away, leaving him to the chore.

I was an adult with children with pets of their own before I considered there was likely a different reality for Snuffles's ultimate demise. Danny White, delicately performing the euthanizing of a rodent? I laugh now at the thought of it! But at that time, seeing my grief, Dad did his best to comfort me by showing me tenderness and by convincing me that my cares were his cares. And it worked. He, Mister Always-Ready-To-Teach-A-Lesson, could've seized that opportunity to educate me about the circle of life. Instead, he recognized that comfort was what I needed and went outside his norm to provide it. As it often is, the lesson was in the experience, anyway.

These two simple experiences, among others, strengthened the bond we would need to endure grief that was to come, a shared grief we certainly never planned on.

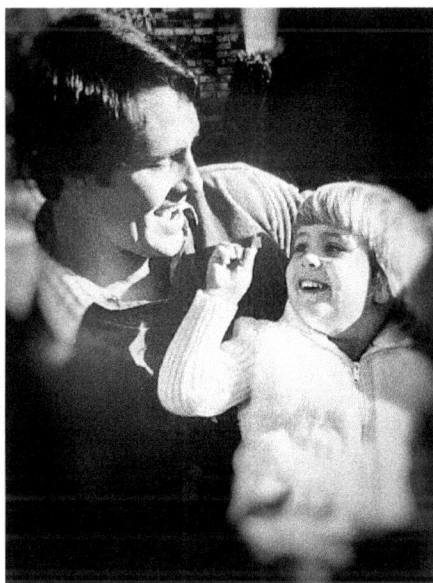

Diagnosis

*"Friendship improves happiness, and abates misery, by the
doubling of our joys, and the dividing of our grief."*
                                    Marcus Tillius Cicero

DW

It was February 2015. We decided to buy a new home
in South Gilbert which caused a broad, unexpected
ripple effect. Realtors convinced us that renovating
our home would be beneficial to the sale, so we began
renovation which caused mass chaos. The stress induced
by the disorder, plus worry about relocating Jo's mom
(who was living with us) caused so much anxiety that it
compounded some symptoms Jo had been having with
vision and coordination. While driving, she had extreme
difficulty and confusion and ended up swiping another

car on the freeway. Then she missed the turn-off to our house. All this pushed her to seek medical help.

She went in to have her vision checked and the eye doctor discovered she had very limited peripheral vision, especially to her left. The vision doctor wanted her to get an MRI, to be safe. The radiologist called our family doctor immediately, who called us and told us to get to Barrows Neurological Institute right away. We were not to go home or pack any bags, just go straight to the hospital.

Barrows took her in immediately and had a room ready when we arrived. They discovered a large mass on the right side of her brain. It looked to be fast growing and malignant...glioblastoma.

At the rate this tumor was growing, time was a significant factor. Had she not been so stressed from the home projects she would have endured her symptoms much longer. Too long.

HJ

Coming out of recovery from her first brain surgery, she provided us with some great entertainment. Dad, the boys, and I were present.

First thing Mom asked was, "Did you find me?"

We assured her that she had been found.

"I was at IHOP," was her reply. Immediately seeing an opportunity for much needed comic relief, we did what any loving family would do—we goaded her.

"What did you order at IHOP, Mom? Did you get extra bacon? How did it taste? What's the combination to the safe?"

Too often in that last month she made us laugh and laughed with us. She kept things light and fun when she was able to. She never had much pain. And she never gave up. She said she wanted to fight the cancer, and when we would ask her to have 'strong legs' she'd repeat, "strong legs, strong legs." We knew she was trying.

About three weeks before her diagnosis and surgery, we started noticing a difference in her personality. It changed so much, like she had gone away somewhere. It's characteristic of the tumor she had. Two days after the tumor was removed, I was on the phone with her while trying to pack up her closet at home. As I heard her voice through the phone, I burst into tears. She was back. She'd been at IHOP, I guess.

Perspective

"It is necessary to go through dark and deeper
dark and not to turn."
Stanley Kunitz

DW

About five months into Jo's bout with brain cancer, our oldest child, Ryan, passed away unexpectedly. Even though Ryan had been born with some heart issues, his death was still unexpected.

He'd had his annual checkup at the Arizona Heart Institute just the day before and was pronounced healthy. So when his wife Helen called us in a panic to tell us that he had collapsed on the sofa while watching TV we were stunned. She had called 911, and they had rushed him to the nearest hospital.

It was determined he needed to be flown to the heart institute where he'd been undergoing long-term observation for his condition. We all drove in separate vehicles to the institute. When Jo arrived, she came to me and asked what had happened because I'd gone to the Emergency Room without her. Not having any confirmation, I had to tell her he had passed out and that it didn't look good.

We got to the hospital and were standing in the hall when the doctor came out and told us that they had him on a machine, and the machine was keeping his heart pumping but there was no brain activity. We needed to decide how long to keep him on the machine.

Knowing he was gone, his wife, Helen, made the decision to take him off right away. I remember my granddaughter, Natalie, Ryan's oldest who was only fourteen at the time, taking her mother by both arms, looking her in the eyes and saying, "We've got this."

HJ

It may seem odd, but I believe mom's cancer was a blessing in this situation. Having just come off radiation, she was in a heavy fog. Though lucid when she called to tell us Ryan had been rushed to the hospital, she wasn't fully herself. I can't imagine the trauma of losing my firstborn, but I think I would welcome a fog.

The Sunday morning Ryan passed was early December. Seeking some solitude and clarity, I went for a walk in the mountains. The day was damp, cold, and gloomy gray. After my walk, I decided to take a peek at some bees I'd been nursing that year, hoping their busy hive would cheer me up. The hive was oddly quiet as I approached. Gently opening their box, I was surprised to see they were all dead.

It was nothing really, in comparison to the loss I felt from Ryan's passing. But the hundreds of lifeless bees in that hushed hive made the shadow of death seem irrevocable. Nothing could be done. Nothing.

One of the hardest days was when we went to the follow up appointment with Mom's oncologist, who said there was nothing more they could do. The words didn't register. You're a doctor, it's what you do. What could she possibly mean? She left the room without any offerings, and we were swallowed up in the emptiness of that word, "nothing."

Desperate for any direction we went back to her surgeon and solicited any and all suggestions. We'd heard of people who went to a cancer clinic in Mexico with miraculous results. The doc didn't like that idea at all, so he threw us a bone. Research trials. There it was. Hope. Something to *do*. As we began looking into the sea of research trials around the country, we quickly discovered the qualifications were far outside Mom's reach. Her cancer was progressing too quickly. Dead end after dead end.

We took her home. The only option left was Mexico, so we started packing, but the whole thing just seemed forced, desperate. It was hurried and sloppy and we just weren't collecting our minds. We called mom's primary care doctor who graciously came to the house to see her. She was calm and levelheaded when she dealt us the blow. "Call hospice."

I'll never forget that moment when we stopped scrambling. We sat in dad's home office. The walls, lined with old photographs and certificates of achievement, the shelves bearing signed footballs and trophies. All those gilded markers of success were lifeless and mocking and of no value to us whatsoever. On the desk sat his laptop with a yellow legal pad filled with scratched out lists of the research trial potentials. The two of us sat frozen, our bags packed in the next room. We could feel something about this trip wasn't right but were reluctant to face reality. We both knew deep down that there was no more sense trying to thwart Mom's prognosis. All we could do was turn to heaven.

This was another time Dad was without words. It was up to me to offer a prayer. I don't remember anything I said or anything we may have heard, but I'll never forget sitting with Dad in that office, tears streaming down both our cheeks as we prayed, hand in hand, for direction. Grief absolutely consumed us. But there was also a peace that can only come from total surrender. The frantic feeling dispersed and a calmness filled the room.

We were done pushing. It was time to hand her over to God.

HJ personal journal entry 12th of August 2016

"Doc says there truly is nothing we can do but make her last little while comfortable. Dad was beside himself. So was I, but I know this was the right choice. So we sat together in his office, just the two of us holding hands, crying, hugging, and said a prayer for confirmation. I don't think there's a worse feeling than this — it's like we're giving up on her. She of all people is worthy of a healing miracle! She has continued to decline but is comfortable and happy. She's been a little funny and is making us laugh. It has been a beautiful and precious experience watching her finish this race. She continues to be an example to me in grace, optimism, priorities, love, and selflessness. She's given me a lifetime of lessons and instead of being bitter and angry for her early departure I hope I can choose gratitude for this beautiful gift God chose to give me... My perfect mother.

Gone to heaven Aug 15, 5am."

DW

It's interesting looking back at the many seeming coincidences. The stress from the house that pushed her symptoms into view. A close family friend of ours who sat on the board at Barrows Institute and said in Jo's situation, there couldn't have been a better facility or surgeon than what she was assigned. The tumor, though large, couldn't have been in a better location. It all just fell into place.

Our lives are filled with blessings. It's up to us to focus our eyes on them. We've kept a journal of all such blessings we received during Jo's last year with us. It includes experiences with her parents and siblings, friends, some remarkable nurses, doctors, and miraculous procedures. Though it's too personal to share publicly, we would be remiss if we didn't acknowledge that when we looked for the hand of God, it was easy to be found. It was her time to go.

HJ

In her passing, Mom gave us each a personal gift.

Reed, being the youngest, had more to lose with Mom's absence in the lives of his young children. During the chaos of the move, she and Dad lived with him and his family. For six months she doted daily on those grandkids whose lives she would soon be the most absent from.

I'm a feely person. It was my opportunity to care for her physically in her final weeks. I can still feel the sensation of her arms around me as I picked her up to move her and dress her. I didn't realize then how valuable that would become when she was gone. It's helped me cope, and I'm so grateful to her for it.

Geoff is a spiritual giant in the family. He kept our perspectives in check when temporal challenges overwhelmed us. As she passed through the veil of mortality, he was there with her, helping Dad give her a spiritual blessing. As she made her transition to heaven, he and Dad were the ones holding her hand.

Those who know Ryan know he was cast from a different mold. He sat the bench and stood in the corners. He struggled in ways we could probably never understand, but Ryan possibly had the best seat in the house when she passed. Forever the last in line, he was likely the first to welcome her Home.

Conclusion

"The man is a success who has lived well, laughed often, and loved much; who has gained the respect of intelligent men and the love of children; who has filled his niche and accomplished his task; who leaves the world better than he found it, whether by an improved poppy, a perfect poem, or a rescued soul; who never lacked appreciation of earth's beauty or failed to express it; who looked for the best in others and gave the best he had."

Robert Louis Stevenson

DW

There are two different kinds of light. One, you should try to get out of, the other, you should try to move toward. As I look back on the experiences I've had with fame, fortune, family, and faith, I've gained insight into the things that matter most. I'm fairly confident God isn't going to need a quarterback in heaven. He may need a piano player though.

The traits I've picked up that will stay with me forever are really all that matter. Replaceable or temporary talents don't mean anything to me now. I spent so much time honing my skills as a football player but was replaced quickly as an athlete when I retired. How much more important is the time I spent developing myself as a father, husband, brother, and friend? Humility, patience, and love will stay with me after those spotlights of fame move on to the next big shot. Most of us have it mixed up. We spend so much time developing temporary talents and not enough time on the permanent ones.

So what? What's the point? Lots of stories and cool

experiences. Who cares? So what? I said in the beginning that I felt an obligation. That because of blessings and opportunities I have received in my life, I want to share and possibly help others who may be struggling with self-esteem or wondering what their purpose in life might be. If I could make one point it would be this. Just because you have not achieved fame and fortune in your life, don't think you're not just as important to the world as anyone else that has lived in it. Just because you have not won any Super Bowls or made a lot of money or had titles like "Quarterback of America's Team," in God's eyes you are as important as anyone.

I've had thousands of people come and go in my life. The accolades and the associations that come with them, as stated earlier, are temporary at best because they come from your status. As soon as the status is gone, they are gone. They are not to be trusted or relied upon. In my opinion, happiness is simply a matter of choosing things and people that *can* be trusted and *can* be relied on. Those things don't require money or status or political, social or financial power.

When you're on the right ladder, it doesn't matter who you know or who you can overcome as you climb to the top. Your success doesn't depend on someone else's failure. The right ladder is wide enough for everybody.

A big part of this new ladder has been my wife, Linda. Linda's husband passed away just a few months after Jo Lynn passed away. She raised five beautiful daughters and has fifteen grandchildren so together we have thirty-one incredible grandchildren. So today, instead of worrying about the right play to run against a 3-2 defense, I'm trying to figure out how to attend a recital and soccer game scheduled at the same time next Saturday.

I hope this book doesn't give the wrong impression about my present life. My state of affairs is fulfilling and even exhilarating, but with much less impressive titles. I'm as happy today as ever. Why? It's not nearly as glamorous as it once was. I don't get invited to every banquet in town or get to hang out with the rich and famous but knowing that the things I am accomplishing with my life right now will never go away makes it all worth it. All of the fluff and the meaningless, temporary stuff that I have spent my life pursuing is being sloughed off. And while it has been incredibly difficult to eliminate from my life all of the labels that have been attached to me like "Dallas Cowboys Quarterback" and "Athlete of the Century," what remains is the real me, the husband, father, grandfather, friend. That's the permanent part of me. Qualities and traits and descriptions that I can "take with me." Had I not come down that first ladder, I would not have been able to start climbing a new one.

> *"Records get broken, and money gets spent, but family, friends, and faith are eternal."*
>
> *DW*

HJ

The experience of that downward climb strengthens us in ways we could never imagine. And the best part is, all the light we gained from previous ladders can stay with us forever.

I don't have a single Danny White QB stat memorized. But I do know exactly where he was and what he said to me when I became a mom. I know that when he gets pulled over for speeding, he's going to be lighthearted with the officer. I know when I need inspiration, he's going to have the right words. I know he won't lose his temper when something goes wrong. And I know there's nothing I can do to lose his love.

It's not over yet. There are many more spotlights and shadows to afflict us, I hope. But I also hope that in those moments of pride I can remember Dad's focus on developing character over credentials, gratitude over greed, and humility during both the highs and lows.

Everyone has something positive to offer this world. It's got nothing to do with a scorecard or a spotlight. It's got everything to do with the light inside.

APPENDIX: Favorite quotes

HJ

As a teenager, I bought Dad a book with blank pages. "Put that in Your Book," was the title on the cover (a quote from *Dances with Wolves*). It was meant to be a little journal of sorts to collect all his favorite quotes. Dad has always been a quote nerd. We love to sit around and take turns rambling off movie quotes to see if each other can "name that movie". He's since filled that little book I gave him. Here are a handful of favorite stories, quotes, and poems he's memorized. Feel free to quiz him, should you ever get the chance.

Right and Wrong

"There's right and there's wrong. You got to do one or the other. You do the one and you're living. You do the other and you may be walking around, but you're dead as a beaver hat."

Davy Crockett played by John Wayne in "The Alamo"

Scratchings from the Little Red Hen

Said the big white rooster, "Gosh, all hemlock, things are tough,
Seems that worms are getting scarce and I cannot find enough.

What's become of all those fat ones is a mystery to me;
There were thousands through the rainy spell, but now where can they be?"

The little red hen, who heard him, didn't grumble or complain,
She had gone through lots of dry spells, she has lived through floods of rain;

So she flew up on the grindstone and she gave her claws a whet,
And she said, "I've never seen a time there were no worms to get."

She picked a new and undug spot; the earth was hard and firm.
The big white rooster jeered, "New ground? That's no place for a worm."

The little red hen spread her feet, she dug fast and free.
"I must go to the worms," she said, "the worms won't come to me."

The rooster vainly spent his day, through habit by the ways,
where fat worms have passed in squads, back in the rainy days.

When nightfall found him supperless, he growled in accents rough,
"I'm hungry as a fowl can be, Conditions sure are tough."

He turned to the little red hen and said, "It's worse with you,
for you're not only hungry, but you must be tired too.

I rested while I watched for worms, so I feel fairly perk;
But how are you? Without worms too? And after all that work?"

The little red hen hopped to her perch and dropped her eyes to sleep,
and murmured, in a drowsy tone, "Young man, hear this and weep,

I'm full of worms and happy, for I've dined both long
and well,
the worms were there, as always—but I had to dig like
hell!"

Oh, here and there white roosters are still holding sales
positions,
they cannot do much business now, because of poor
conditions.

But as soon as things get right again, they'll sell a hundred
firms—
Meanwhile, the little red hens are out, a-gobbling up the
worms.

Stewart Miller

The Sportsman's Prayer

Dear Lord, in the battle that goes on through life, I ask
but a field that is fair, a chance that is equal with all in the
strife, the courage to strive and to dare. If I should win,
let it be by the code, with my faith and my honor held
high. If I should lose, let me stand by the road and cheer
as the winners go by.

Berton Braley

Princes and Kings

Isn't it strange how princes and kings,
and clowns that caper in sawdust rings,
and common people, like you and me,
are builders for eternity?

Each is given a list of rules;
a shapeless mass; a bag of tools.
And each must fashion, ere life is flown,
A stumbling block, or a Stepping-Stone."

R. Lee Sharpe

The Ambulance Down in the Valley

'Twas a dangerous cliff, as they freely confessed,
Though to walk near its crest was so pleasant;
But over its terrible edge there had slipped
A duke and full many a peasant.

So the people said something would have to be done,
But their projects did not at all tally;
Some said, "Put a fence 'round the edge of the cliff,"
Some, "An ambulance down in the valley."

But the cry for the ambulance carried the day,
For it spread through the neighboring city;
A fence may be useful or not, it is true,
But each heart became full of pity

For those who slipped over the dangerous cliff;
And the dwellers in highway and alley
Gave pounds and gave pence, not to put up a fence,
But an ambulance down in the valley.

"For the cliff is all right, if you're careful," they said,
"And, if folks even slip and are dropping,
It isn't the slipping that hurts them so much
As the shock down below when they're stopping."

So day after day, as these mishaps occurred,
Quick forth would those rescuers sally
To pick up the victims who fell off the cliff,
With their ambulance down in the valley.

Then an old sage remarked: "It's a marvel to me
That people give far more attention
To repairing results than to stopping the cause,
When they'd much better aim at prevention.

Let us stop at its source all this mischief," cried he,
"Come, neighbors and friends, let us rally;
If the cliff we will fence, we might almost dispense
With the ambulance down in the valley."

"Oh he's a fanatic," the others rejoined,
"Dispense with the ambulance? Never!
He'd dispense with all charities, too, if he could;
No! No! We'll support them forever.

Aren't we picking up folks just as fast as they fall?
And shall this man dictate to us? Shall he?
Why should people of sense stop to put up a fence,
While the ambulance works in the valley?"

But the sensible few, who are practical too,
Will not bear with such nonsense much longer;
They believe that prevention is better than cure,
And their party will soon be the stronger.

Encourage them then, with your purse, voice, and pen,
And while other philanthropists dally,
They will scorn all pretense, and put up a stout fence
On the cliff that hangs over the valley.

Better guide well the young than reclaim them when old,
For the voice of true wisdom is calling.
"To rescue the fallen is good, but 'tis best
To prevent other people from falling."

Better close up the source of temptation and crime
Than deliver from dungeon or galley;
Better put a strong fence 'round the top of the cliff
Than an ambulance down in the valley.

Joseph Malins

With Coach the day he was fired.

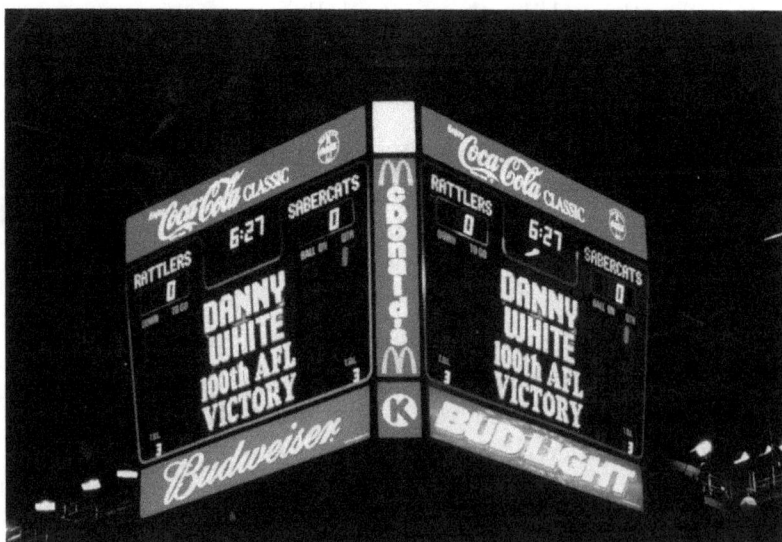

Promo picture with Tony Dorsett.
They called us Ebony and Ivory.

Me and Linda with our new team!

Acknowledgments

DW

I want to dedicate this book to the members of all the teams that have made it possible, who have shared this journey with me by pushing, pulling, guiding or just being there for me. First of all, family, including, Jo Lynn, my parents and in-laws, Jane, Linda, Ryan and Helen, Geoff and Andrea, Heather and Kelly, Reed and Hailey, Teresa and Rich, Tammy and Scott, Cristall and Mark, Chad and Michele. As well as all my grandchildren and extended family. Also, my close friends, who have convinced me that their friendship is not a result of my titles. And all my teammates and friends from Edison Elementary School to Kino Junior High School to Westwood High School, to the Arizona Rattlers, to the Utah Blaze, to the Dallas Cowboys and beyond.

Danny White is best known for his thirteen season NFL career with the Dallas Cowboys. Danny led Dallas to the playoffs five times, including three straight appearances in the NFC Championship Game and two Super Bowls. He finished his career as the franchise's most accurate passer and all-time leader in both completions and touchdown passes. He still holds several Cowboys' records including most TD passes thrown in Texas Stadium.

An All-American at Arizona State University, Danny set seven NCAA passing records and was named Sports Illustrated's second-highest rated quarterback of all time. White finished his college career as the NCAA's all-time leading passer, one of seven national passing records he set at ASU.

After retiring from the NFL in 1988, White was a head coach in the Arena Football League for 15 seasons, making 15 playoff appearances and leading the Arizona Rattlers to five Arena Bowls. He won the Arena League Championship twice.

In addition to the AFL Hall of Fame and the NCAA Hall of Fame, White has been inducted into the Mesa Arizona Sports Hall of Fame, the State of Arizona Sports Hall of Fame, and the Arizona State University Hall of Fame where his jersey, number 11, was retired. White was also named the Arizona Athlete of the Century by the Arizona Republic in 2000. In 2024 he was presented with the Davey O'Brien Legend award.

Danny is currently the analyst for Compass Media, broadcasting all Dallas Cowboy games over their nationally syndicated networks and travels as an inspirational public speaker. He lives in Mesa, Arizona with his wife Linda. Together they have nine children and thirty-one grandchildren. Sixteen of those are Danny's. (Roger only has fifteen.)

www.dannywhite.com

Heather Jo Kennedy is a Certified Professional Life Coach and inspirational public speaker like her father. She speaks to teams of all industries about the importance of their relationships and shares lessons she's learned from growing up under the influence of "America's Team". She has fond memories of growing up in Texas with her parents and three brothers. The family moved to Arizona when she was fourteen. Her senior year of high school she was titled Arizona's Junior Miss in 1997 and represented her state at the national program. After graduating Cum Laude from Utah State University, Heather and her husband started several businesses which are still in operation along the Utah Wasatch Front. They enjoy their rural living, where they are raising their four children.

www.hjkennedy.com

www.ingramcontent.com/pod-product-compliance
Lightning Source LLC
Chambersburg PA
CBHW071431090426
42737CB00011B/1629